When a Crisis Hits

Will Your School Be Ready?

Robert H. Decker

CORWIN PRESS, INC.
A Sage Publications Company
Thousand Oaks, California

Copyright © 1997 by Corwin Press, Inc.

All rights reserved. No part of this book may be reproduced or utilized in any form or by any means, electronic or mechanical, including photocopying, recording, or by any information storage and retrieval system, without permission in writing from the publisher.

For information:

Corwin Press, Inc.
A Sage Publications Company
2455 Teller Road
Thousand Oaks, California 91320
E-mail: order@corwin.sagepub.com

SAGE Publications Ltd.
6 Bonhill Street
London EC2A 4PU
United Kingdom

SAGE Publications India Pvt. Ltd.
M-32 Market
Greater Kailash I
New Delhi 110 048 India

Library of Congress Cataloging-in-Publication Data

Decker, Robert H.
  When a crisis hits: Will your school be ready? / by Robert H. Decker.
    p. cm.
  Includes bibliographical references.
  ISBN 0-8039-6615-6 (cloth : acid-free paper). — ISBN 0-8039-6304-1 (pbk. : acid-free paper)
  1. School crisis management—United States.　I. Title.
LB2866.5.D43 1997
363.11'9371—dc21　　　　　　　　　　　　　　97-4896

This book is printed on acid-free paper.

99 00 01 02 03 10 9 8 7 6 5 4 3 2

Editorial Assistant: Kristen L. Gibson
Production Editor: Sanford Robinson
Production Assistant: Karen Wiley
Typesetter/Designer: Danielle Dillahunt
Cover Designer: Marcia R. Finlayson

Contents

Preface	vi
Acknowledgments	viii
About the Author	x

PART ONE:
10-Step Approach to Developing a Crisis Plan

1. **Should Your School Have a Crisis Plan?** — 3
   - What Is a Crisis? — 3
   - Step 1: Establish a District Policy and a Safety and Crisis Management Mission Statement — 5
   - Why a School Must Address a Crisis — 5

2. **Parts of the Planning Process** — 8
   - Step 2: Appoint a Districtwide Task Force — 8
   - Step 3: Survey Surrounding School Districts as Well as Your Own — 10
   - Step 4: Conduct Assessment of Building Security — 10
   - Step 5: Identify Current and Proposed Safety Features — 18

3. **The Safety and Crisis Management Team** — 22
   - Step 6: Identify, Designate, and Document the Safety and Crisis Management Team — 22

4. **The Plan** — 31
   - Step 7: Set Goals and Guidelines for Developing Building-Level Plans — 32
   - Step 8: Develop a "Table of Contents" for the Building Safety and Crisis Management Plan — 33
   - Step 9: Develop a Safety and Crisis Management Plan — 35
   - Step 10: Distribute the Safety and Crisis Management Plan — 47

PART TWO:
Critical Components for Dealing With Crises

5. Being Sensitive to Student and Staff Needs — 51
- Addressing the Needs of Staff and Students—Faculty Responsibilities — 52
- Students' Reactions to Crisis Situations — 53
- Allowing Students to Attend Memorial or Funeral Services — 54
- Half-Mast Flag Guidelines — 56
- When Informing the Media — 56

6. Prevention Programs and Strategies — 58
- Preparing the Faculty to Deal With Crime and Violence — 59
- The Use of Sweeps and Searches — 60
- The Use of Metal Detectors — 61
- Vandalism in the Building or on Campus — 63
- Developing a Student Assistance Program — 65
- Linking to Law Enforcement Agencies — 73
- Breaking Up Fights — 76
- Student Anger and Violence — 78
- Prevention Strategies — 82
- School and District Response Strategies — 83

7. Including Parents as Partners in Prevention — 85
- A Community Concern — 85
- First Step for Parents — 86
- Three Types of Parents — 86
- Concerns of Parents — 88
- Strategies to Help Parents Become Involved — 89
- Schools Building Bridges With Parents — 89
- Community Patrons Can Help Too — 91
- The School's Role — 91

8. Bringing Conflict Management Into the School — 95
- Understanding Conflict in an Educational Sense — 95
- Ask These Questions When Looking at Conflict Types — 98
- What About Resolution? — 98
- Implementing a Conflict Resolution Program in Your School — 100

9. Being Proactive in Dealing With Gangs — 104

   Gangs Are Not Only an Urban Problem — 105
   Schools as Enablers — 105
   How Gangs Evolve — 106
   Gang Clothing and Other Markings (Symbols) — 106
   Gang Mythology — 107
   Take a Gang Assessment Survey — 109
   Gang Assessment and Planning Guide — 111
   Characteristics of a Successful Prevention Program — 112
   Recommendations for Parents and Educators — 113
   Areas of Concern Related to Gangs and Safe Schools — 113
   School Discipline When Gangs or Gang Members Are Involved — 115
   Be Proactive in Keeping Your School Safe — 116
   Participant Roles in School Safety Planning — 117
   Additional Strategies for Establishing a Safe School — 117

Resource A: Crisis Situations and Anticipated Response — 120

References — 174

CORWIN PRESS

The Corwin Press logo—a raven striding across an open book—represents the happy union of courage and learning. We are a professional-level publisher of books and journals for K–12 educators, and we are committed to creating and providing resources that embody these qualities. Corwin's motto is "Success for All Learners."

Preface

This guide contains all the necessary components for a school's administration to become proactive in its quest to develop a comprehensive crisis management plan. As our society has changed and continues to change as to acceptable and unacceptable behavior, school administrators find themselves in both difficult straits and legal entanglements when administering schools during times of crisis. The building administrator should not be the only person involved during a crisis. Teachers, staff, other administrators, community patrons, and local community agencies all play an important part in providing assistance when a crisis hits.

This how-to book takes you through a step-by-step process to building a crisis management plan that works. The many examples given provide a guide for clarity, or developers can use the examples to check the school's existing plan to see if it is complete. *When a Crisis Hits: Will Your School Be Ready?* helps to minimize the possibility that administrators, faculty, or staff will make "fatal errors" during or after a crisis. Chapter 1 sets the stage for the whole process. Developing a policy and understanding the philosophical underpinnings is where a school building or district needs to begin. Having the leadership to share the vision of this important process is crucial to developing a first-rate plan. As a plan is developed, the administration will become aware of the need for staff development and training that goes along with crisis management planning.

Chapter 2 starts readers on their way to the planning process. It answers the questions: Why do we need a crisis management plan? Who needs to be involved on a crisis team? What are the components of a crisis plan? Many examples are given to assist the reader in the variations that can be developed as they relate to your possibly unique situation. By understanding the basic premise and guiding principles, an administration can develop a process that will work and one that community, students, and parents will appreciate if your school or district becomes involved in a crisis.

Chapter 3 zeros in on the function of the crisis team. It answers the questions: What is the purpose of the crisis team? What is the procedure to follow given a crisis situation? What are the faculty and staff roles during a crisis situation? What happens after a crisis situation? This book enables the practitioner to anticipate and respond to questions that faculty, community, and others may have as the plan is being developed.

Chapter 4 assists the development team in actually putting a plan together. Information is given, with examples, to help your district identify concerns and potential problem areas. With the help of examples, your team will be able to develop a plan and be confident that it will be able to handle a crisis situation.

Chapter 5 covers a critical component that is omitted from too many crisis plans: the special needs of individuals who are coping with grief and possibly resolving a loss. Requests will often be made to use building or district facilities for memorial services or to use the facility to have a memorial presented for future remembrance. There may be no policy to cover such occurrences or events, and Chapter 5 helps the administration take a look at establishing appropriate guidelines.

Chapter 6 identifies areas in which training needs to take place and why. School personnel could put themselves in jeopardy and become entangled in legal issues without the proper training and development. Personal injury could result if an employee were to make an error in judgment, especially if the judgment resulted in some form of physical restraint or provocation. Today's classrooms, hallways, cafeterias, and parking lots are used for more than just educational experiences. Proper supervision, not only by administrators, is needed to reduce the amount of vandalism and crime that may be occurring on your campus. All staff members need to assist in supervising students, but many do not want to get involved because they have not been trained in proper techniques or how to handle difficult situations.

Chapter 7 is critical to the administrators who find themselves in the midst of vandalism, crime, and violent behavior. Community patrons and parents of students will also see many of these same behaviors in the community and the home. Questions and comments on what should be done will start to surface and answers will be sought. The school administration may be one of the first places people will look for answers and guidance. This chapter will help the administration guide the community, and more closely, parents, in identifying and dealing with potentially difficult and explosive situations. Also, this chapter will enable administrators to develop a positive and proactive way of connecting to the community and, more important, with the parents of students.

Chapter 8 clarifies the area of conflict management and how it can be incorporated into a school setting. This chapter identifies skills needed to become a conflict mediator and how students can assist in keeping the building and campus peaceful and productive. It is important for both students and staff to learn how to defuse difficult, emotional, and stressful situations. Managing conflict before it becomes a crisis is an important proactive process that schools need to develop and implement.

Many communities, whether urban, suburban, or even rural, are concerned with gangs and gang development. Gangs, once thought to be an urban or suburban problem, today exist in virtually every community or geographical area. Some communities may deny the existence of gangs or define groups in some other way, but communities need to become involved if any group's activity turns violent or destructive. Chapter 9 helps the reader become aware of gang development and activity. It will enable the reader to face concerned parents and community members who will have tough questions about school safety when a gang-related crisis hits. Being prepared is a big part of being an educational leader in today's schools and society. You need to understand how to control violence and look objectively at the existing condition of your building or campus.

Finally, Resource A presents three dozen examples of crisis management planning. These examples vividly demonstrate how schools and districts determine what should be in a crisis plan.

This book has been written with compassion for all educators concerned about the devastating effects that crises can have on students, staff, and community. As an administrator, you cannot afford to commit an error when a crisis hits. Emotions run high and tolerance for poor judgment is low during a time of need and anguish. Being proactive and prepared to meet the challenge of a crisis is the first step in eliminating fatal errors. With these thoughts in mind, I hope you will reflect on the ideas, processes, and strategies emphasized in these pages, but most of all, I hope your school will be prepared to deal with the crisis when it hits.

Acknowledgments

I would like to thank the many people who helped bring this book to fruition, especially Gary Ray of Ray and Associates, Inc. Without his help, encouragement, and assistance, this book would not have been completed. My thanks also go to Richard Hinojosa, a gang prevention counselor in the Houston area, for all his insight and for allowing me to use some of his information, and to Chuck Broawner, chief of police for the Spring Branch Independent School District, Houston, for his assistance in making this book possible.

I gratefully acknowledge the assistance of both the Spring Branch and Eagle Mountain–Saginaw Independent School Districts in the state of Texas for granting me permission to use some of their crisis management information as models for other school districts. Both Superintendent Hal Guthrie of Spring Branch and Public Relations Officer Julie Thannum of Eagle Mountain–Saginaw were extremely helpful.

I am indebted to many subscribers of the K-12admin listserv on the Internet who chose to share information, scenarios, and situations as this book was being developed. Much insight and leadership were shared by some great administrators across the United States and Canada.

Finally, I would like to acknowledge the professional colleagues and friends who provided motivation and encouragement to write this book, Ed Chance at the University of Nevada–Las Vegas and colleagues at the

University of Northern Iowa; the many students in my administration classes who provided feedback and criticism so this book could be a practical application for the profession; and my dear students in western Iowa who offered insight, enthusiasm, and encouragement as well.

Without the help of so many people, this book would have been difficult to develop. My sincere thanks and great appreciation for all their assistance. I would be most ungrateful if I did not thank my wife, Paula, and our children, who have weathered the crisis of a husband and dad writing a book. With five grown and two almost-grown children, I have experienced a number of crises over the years. (At one time I was blessed to have four teenagers in the same house at the same time; now *that* is a crisis!) And you know, we got through it without committing any fatal errors. With a little forethought, some good information, and many blessings, anything is possible.

ROBERT H. DECKER

About the Author

Robert H. Decker is Associate Professor in the College of Education, Department of Educational Leadership, Counseling and Postsecondary Education at the University of Northern Iowa. He has been a teacher, coach, secondary school principal, and associate superintendent in both the private and public school systems. He received his degrees from Chicago State University, Southern Illinois University–Carbondale, Southeast Missouri State University, and Illinois State University. His diverse background in urban, suburban, and rural education has given him the benefit of being involved in numerous educational environments and many crisis situations.

He is author or coauthor of more than 40 articles and manuscripts in the areas of educational leadership, management, technology, and educational supervision. Based on his professional experience, he has become known as an authority in educational management decision making and crisis management program prevention. He has spent a great deal of his professional career in developing and understanding crisis management decision making and policy formulation.

Decker has conducted more than 100 consultations, workshops, and presentations to international groups, national and state conferences, local organizations, and schools. He continues to work with boards of education on management issues and leadership training. As a consultant he has worked with teachers, administrators, and community groups to assist in the development of crisis management plans and procedures. He has owned his own company and has consulted with major corporations in the area of educational technology.

At the present, besides being an associate professor, he is the National Director in the consulting firm of Ray and Associates, Inc., which consults with both public and private agencies on various educational issues. Many consultations involve personnel, management, and crisis decision-making situations.

Part One

10-Step Approach to Developing a Crisis Plan

Chapter One

Should Your School Have a Crisis Plan?

It was Sunday evening when the telephone rang; the voice on the other end said that the high school was ablaze. The fire was rated a 4-11 (the most severe), and by the time you arrived, three fourths of the building had been totally destroyed. As high school principal, you were starting to be barraged with questions from community individuals and parents as to where classes were going to be held and when.

What should you do, and how would you respond?

Experience has taught us that a school crisis may occur at any time and strike with varying degrees of severity. In the event of a crisis situation, calm, responsible personnel and reactions are essential to the effective management of the emergency. A situation such as the one above causes stress and hardship on administrators, and administrators must be prepared to handle a multitude of situations that might constitute a crisis within a school.

What Is a Crisis?

Webster's Collegiate Dictionary describes a *crisis* as an emotionally significant event or radical change; an unstable or crucial time, or state of affairs in which a decisive change is impending. When we look at a school crisis, we identify any event that drastically disrupts or alters a normal school day.

A school crisis may include any of the following situations (not an exhaustive list):

- Loss of electrical power (for example, a person trapped in an elevator)

- Campus fire/building damage
- Toxic chemical spill
- School evacuation/relocation of students
- Student/teacher death
- School bus accident
- Injuries on campus
- Suicide or threat of suicide
- Crime on campus: assault, robbery, rape, gang activity
- Violence on or near campus: gang fight, beating, riot, stabbing/cutting, shooting, homicide
- Terroristic activity: bomb threat, hostage situation
- Explosion: boiler room, science lab
- Natural disasters: severe thunderstorm, flood, tornado, hurricane, earthquake
- Drive-by shooting/multiple-injury violence
- Campus intruder: trespasser, deranged person, armed person
- Campus unrest: Student/teacher/parent protest or walkout, racial tension
- Teacher/employee arrested for drugs, sex offense, serious violence, and so on

All across America, schools have had to manage crises or tragic situations that have occurred on their campuses. Virtually all schools have some type of plan in place for a natural disaster such as a tornado, fire, hurricane, or flood. It is becoming mandatory that schools be prepared for a multitude of other potential school crises. It is essential to the safety and welfare of every campus that a practical and workable safety and crisis management plan be developed by each school building in the school district. More important, amid the violence of today it is a necessity for every campus to have a safety and crisis management team that is competent, capable, and adequately prepared to handle an emergency situation. Furthermore, all staff members must know their roles in a crisis and do their part. The campus administrator must encourage familiarization of the staff with the plan developed specifically for that school.

School authorities have both a moral obligation and a legal responsibility to provide for protection of public property and the life, health, and property of students, faculty, and staff in emergencies.

The safety and crisis management plan should consist of a 10-step approach for handling crises or tragic situations. These 10 steps will guide the building or campus through most crises and tragic situations. Figure 1.1 identifies the 10 steps, and the remainder of Chapters 1, 2, 3, 4, and 5 will assist the building committee in establishing an in-depth and

Step 1	Establish a district policy and a safety and crisis management mission statement
Step 2	Appoint a districtwide task force
Step 3	Survey surrounding school districts as well as your own
Step 4	Conduct assessment of building security
Step 5	Identify current and proposed safety features
Step 6	Identify, designate, and document the safety and crisis management team
Step 7	Set goals and guidelines for developing building-level plans
Step 8	Develop a "table of contents" for the building safety and crisis management plan
Step 9	Develop a safety and crisis management plan
Step 10	Distribute the safety and crisis management plan

Figure 1.1. Overall Safety and Crisis Management Plan

valuable document that all hope will never have to be put into operation. However, if the safety and crisis management plan has to be implemented, be sure that the team, with support from the faculty, staff, and community, is prepared to meet whatever challenge comes its way.

Step 1: Establish a District Policy and a Safety and Crisis Management Mission Statement

One of your first priorities to legitimize your plan is to get your school board to establish a board policy/mission statement on safe schools. This directive will send the message to students, staff, and community that the district believes school safety is a top priority so that consistent prevention and response measures are available on demand. Furthermore, this creates a trickle-down effect of safety from the board of education to students, staff, parents, and community.

As with many significant school-related matters, a board policy is recommended to put the educational community on notice that the school district intends to deal with situations and procedures as they come up and are needed in the effective and efficient administration of the school district. Having a crisis management policy statement sends a clear message to the district constituency of the awareness of dangerous and traumatic situations that may occur while their children attend school. Figure 1.2 is an example of a board policy statement regarding safety and crisis management planning that might be developed by a school district after considerable thought and discussion. It is also suggested that the district's legal counsel or state school board association review any policy regarding school safety or crisis management.

Why a School Must Address a Crisis

Our society has changed over the past several decades, and we now live in a society that is becoming increasingly complex and volatile. We can no longer routinely think that crisis situations happen only to others or

USA School District
PROPOSED CRISIS MANAGEMENT POLICY

The USA School District believes that crisis management planning is a major priority in providing a safe and secure environment for students and staff. Crisis planning requires a collaborative effort of the Board of Education, administrators, teachers, students, parents, and community. A variety of prevention and intervention strategies, programs, and activities must be in place to ensure student and staff welfare.

A comprehensive, concise, and specific plan shall be developed and coordinated to cover emergencies and will consist of a plan for each public elementary and secondary school in the USA School District.

Plans will include an organization chart with lines of succession and emergency assignments clearly designated. Consideration must be given to security and preservation of essential records and sensitive areas such as boiler rooms and electrical panels.

The emergency procedure must be reviewed and updated annually prior to the commencement of school. This shall be done with input from building administrators, central administration, and others appropriate to the evaluation of such plans.

Figure 1.2. Step 1: Sample Policy Statement

that disasters happen only in other parts of the state or country. There is overwhelming evidence that crisis situations will probably occur in your building within the next 3 to 5 years, if not sooner. Is your school district (building) ready to deal with a crisis situation?

When school personnel are prepared to deal with a crisis, students can continue to grow emotionally, intellectually, and physically. Divisiveness and further trauma can be averted. With proper preparation, a crisis can be used to unite students and staff in building confidence and cohesiveness among themselves and within the larger public community.

There are opportunities that exist in a crisis. It does not have to be a totally traumatic experience. It is possible for the school to bring students together, forming a sense of community that only comes from a deep sharing. A school will not realize this benefit by taking a "business as usual" approach to a crisis situation or personal tragedy.

Because it is difficult to make all the decisions necessary to contain the crisis and channel the emotional reactions on the day of an event, preplanning will be your greatest asset. With the help of this book, it is hoped that you, the educational administrator in charge of maintaining an educational environment and providing for the health and welfare of your students, will be able to assist your staff in developing a safety and crisis management plan that will reduce trauma and emotional distress and at the same time build a sense of community in difficult times.

The administrator who can be proactive and foresee the future is the individual who will be perceived to be an effective administrator. As we have learned in education, perception is reality for many of our constituency.

As an administrator and as a school district, you do not want to commit the "fatal error" of not being ready when a crisis hits. When a crisis hits, it is too late to be proactive; at that point all you can do is hold on and react to the situation, increasing your ability to make the fatal error for which you will be eternally remembered.

Chapter Two

Parts of the Planning Process

It was 1:34 p.m. Wednesday afternoon when the city sirens went off, alerting everyone of an approaching dangerous storm. Principal Michael Jurgensen took the needed precautions and had the staff of his elementary building take the students to appropriate safety locations until the storm had passed. At 1:57 p.m. a tornado moved through the town and hit the elementary school. There was mass destruction with some severe injuries and possible deaths.

If this happened in your school, what would you do?

All across America, school officials have found themselves in situations that require them to manage a crisis or tragic situation that has occurred at their school campuses. Most schools have plans in place for certain events such as fire and flood. It is only natural that school districts expand their preparedness drills for other potential school-related crises. It is essential to the safety and welfare of every campus that a practical and workable safety and crisis management plan is developed by every building or campus in a school district.

Step 2: Appoint a Districtwide Task Force

When starting to develop a schoolwide safety and crisis management plan and after developing a board policy and/or mission statement, a districtwide task force needs to be identified and meetings conducted to assist the district in appraising available community services and assistance. This committee should plan the safety measures that are necessary for the district for three important reasons. First, building principals can consistently apply practical prevention techniques. Second, people support what they create, and by getting all groups involved, from board members to students, all will support the goals of the school. The prem-

Parts of the Planning Process 9

ise that people support what they help to create is a very powerful force at this stage of development. Third, once the districtwide task force has completed its role, district administrators fulfill an advisory role to educate safety and crisis management teams and provide the necessary support at the district level during crisis and postcrisis situations.

The size of the task force will be determined by each district and the resources that are available to it. It is suggested that the task force be limited to a planning committee of 8 to 10 individuals. The task force members may be appointed from some of the following community and school-related areas.

Community services. Individuals representing human service organization(s) are excellent in providing potential services in the event of a crisis.

Law enforcement. A representative of the local police department (community service representative) can advise the district as to appropriate reporting procedures.

School security officer. If your school has a security officer or campus security department, a representative would greatly enhance the knowledge base as to potential problems or crisis situations.

District and site administrators. Depending on the size of the district, district and site administrators need to be involved in the discussion involving district crime and crisis potential.

Staff. Representatives from the staff will bring a different perspective to the task force. Also, it is important to communicate with individuals who will be directly involved in implementing whatever final safety and crisis management plan is developed.

Students. Many times, we lose sight of the student perspective. It is important that students of appropriate age be given the opportunity to have input into discussions that quite possibly will affect them later. It is also very important to have a student resource when situations call for information that is widely known only by students.

Parents. Parents should be an important part of the initial discussion concerning safety and crisis management planning. Communication to parents is vital in crisis situations. Parents can be advocates and assist the district as they develop an ownership in the planning process. They will also be positive public relation proponents for the district.

Others. The potential for the district resources should be assessed, and the individuals you believe will help in identifying and planning for a crisis situation should be invited.

Most important, amid the violence today it is a necessity for every district to have a task force team that is competent, capable, and adequately prepared to discuss and handle an emergency situation. In addition to the task force team, all staff persons must know their roles in a crisis and do their part. The campus administrator must encourage familiarization of his or her staff with the plan developed specifically for their school. In fact, on a sporadic basis, the district needs to provide crisis drills to monitor the procedures of each building and to alert the district and building crisis teams to any vulnerable points in their plans.

Step 3: Survey Surrounding School Districts as Well as Your Own

Many crises have the potential of happening on school campuses today. There are not only natural disasters as described at the beginning of this chapter but also other situations that develop from criminal acts and tragic accidents. With the amount of crime on school campuses today, there is a need to be proactive in preparing to deal with the situation. Figure 2.1 is an assessment tool for administrators to use to evaluate the vulnerability of their campus concerning school crime. The tool assesses the school climate, which allows school administrators the opportunity to identify and address potential dangerous situations. Use this assessment tool to indicate potential problems; it should not be viewed as the final verdict on campus climate.

Along with evaluating your own campus, it is wise to assess surrounding school districts in regard to what they are doing with safety and crisis management planning and preparation. It is not important for your district to be original; it *is* important for your district to be prepared to handle as many potential crisis situations as possible. As a resource tool to investigate security and crisis management measures of surrounding school districts, a survey provides contacts from those districts. The School Security and Crisis Management Survey (Figure 2.2) will provide vital information to the district task force. This will aid in giving direction for the district safety and crisis management model and guidelines that will be implemented on the school building level.

Step 4: Conduct Assessment of Building Security

Once the crisis team has been defined, roles and procedures set, and the School Security and Crisis Management Survey completed, an assessment of the building security needs to take place. The Building Security Assessment Checklist (Figure 2.3) will assist the school or campus in completing a thorough crime prevention inspection. This checklist was designed to gather valuable security information about the school site, the existing security system, building or campus perimeter surroundings, and building or campus exterior and interior surroundings. By using this checklist, you will have the necessary information to make informed decisions concerning the safety of equipment and students at all

Parts of the Planning Process 11

Many schools are surrounded by a 360-degree perimeter of community crime. The National School Safety Center (NSSC) has developed the following School Crime Assessment Tool to assist school administrators in evaluating their vulnerability to school crime issues and potential school climate problems. The results of this review will provide school administrators with a clear idea of districtwide priorities that should be addressed. Answer yes or no to the following questions.

- ___ Has your community crime rate increased over the past 12 months?
- ___ Are more than 15 percent of your work order repairs vandalism related?
- ___ Do you have an open campus?
- ___ Has an underground student newspaper recently emerged?
- ___ Is your community transiency rate increasing?
- ___ Do you have an increasing presence of graffiti in your community?
- ___ Do you have an increased presence of gangs in your community?
- ___ Is your truancy rate increasing?
- ___ Are your suspension and expulsion rates increasing?
- ___ Have you experienced increased conflicts among students relative to dress style, food services, and types of music played at special events?
- ___ Do you have an increasing number of students on probation at your school?
- ___ Have you had isolated, racially motivated fights?
- ___ Have you reduced the number of extracurricular programs and sports at your school?
- ___ Are parents withdrawing students from your school because of fear?
- ___ Has your budget for professional development opportunities and inservice training for your staff been reduced or eliminated?
- ___ Are you discovering more weapons on your campus?
- ___ Do you lack written screening and selection guidelines for new teachers and other youth-serving professionals who work in your school?
- ___ Are drugs easily available in or around your school?
- ___ Does your annual staff turnover exceed 25 percent?
- ___ Have you had a student demonstration or other signs of unrest within the past 12 months?

Scoring

Multiply each affirmative answer by 5, and add the total.

Interpretation

0 to 20	No significant school safety problem.
25 to 45	You have an emerging school safety problem and should develop a safe school plan.
50 to 70	There is significant potential for school safety problems. A safe school plan should be developed.
75 and up	You are sitting on a time bomb. Begin working on your safe school plan immediately. Get outside help.

Figure 2.1. NSSC School Crime Assessment Tool

SOURCE: Developed by Dr. Ronald D. Stephens, Executive Director, National School Safety Center, Pepperdine University, Malibu, CA 90265. Used with permission.

1. Do you have an organized security program for your school/district?

    Yes _____   No _____

    If not, is it something that has been considered?

    Why or why not?

    If so, what are the most and least successful measures you have used?

2. Do you limit access to the schools in any way? (e.g., locked doors, security personnel, metal detectors). Please elaborate.

3. Do you have I.D. cards for students and staff?

    Yes _____   No _____

4. Do you check I.D. on people entering the building?

    Yes _____   No _____

5. Do you use security personnel?

    Yes _____   No _____

    If so, please let us know who, when, and how (e.g., local police or school system employees, during school, before and after school, social events, athletic events, inside the building, outside the building, uniformed or not, how visible to students, etc.)

6. Based on your experiences, what recommendations would you make to other schools?

7. What do you feel is the single, most effective safety and prevention measure?

    Your response to this survey is greatly appreciated. If you would like a copy of the results of this survey, please complete the information below:

    Name: _____

    Position: _____

    School/district: _____

    Address/Zip: _____

    Please return survey in the enclosed envelope.

Figure 2.2. School Security and Crisis Management Survey

hours, day or night, and have valuable information regarding the strengths and weaknesses of the current educational site.

Each administrator may want to alter the checklist to make it relevant to his or her district. Due to different environments and geographical

(text continued on page 18)

Parts of the Planning Process 13

Give your school a thorough crime prevention inspection now. Use this checklist as a guideline to determine your school's strengths and weaknesses.

	Yes	No

Organization

1. Is there a formal incident reporting system?
   Is this available to students and teachers?
   Is this being used by the principal?
   Are these being monitored and evaluated?
   Is this information available to the community/parents?

2. Is this information reaching the central district office?

3. Is there statistical information available as to the scope of the problems in your school and in the community?

4. Is there a policy for dealing with violence and vandalism in your school?

5. Is there a policy regarding control and access to the school?
   Is there a visitor procedure?
   Are there signs directing visitors to the main office?
   Is there a trained person *always* available to challenge visitors/make them sign in?
   Are all exits except the main entrance closed during school hours?
   Are there trained personnel monitoring all doors when open?
   Do some members of the custodial staff work nights and weekends?
   Do students have I.D. cards or other identification?
   Do all employees have I.D. cards?
   Is there a policy for intruders, those who loiter, or nonstudents on campus?

6. Is there a policy that limits search and seizures?
   Are all staff members aware of these limits/liabilities?

7. Is there a policy to detect and control or eliminate drugs and weapons?

8. Are the teachers and administrators aware of the laws that pertain to them? To their rights? To students' rights? To their responsibility as to the enforcement of and respect of rules, regulations, policies, and the law?

9. Is there any inservice training available for teachers in the areas of violence and vandalism and other required reporting procedures? (There must be training on all levels.)

10. Are students aware of expectations and school discipline codes?
    Are parents aware?

Figure 2.3. Building Security Assessment Checklist

	Yes	No
11. Are there any actual or contingency action plans developed to deal with student disruptions, vandalism, and graffiti?	___	___
12. Is there a policy to deal with vandalism and graffiti?	___	___
13. Is there a policy as to restitution or prosecution of perpetrators of violence and vandalism?	___	___
Whenever possible, is vandal damage repaired immediately?	___	___
Do job descriptions include vandalism prevention duties?	___	___
Through as many channels as possible, are vandalism costs made known to taxpayers?	___	___
14. Is there training available for teachers in the areas of violence—both verbal and physical—and standard crime prevention?	___	___
15. Is there a policy to keep staff up to date on safety issues and/or violence in the school and community?	___	___
16. Are there specific staff assigned or trained in security awareness?	___	___
What type of ongoing training do the staff receive?	___	___
Do they know how to break up fights?	___	___
Do they know how to diffuse a potentially violent situation?	___	___
Do they know how to speak so students will listen?	___	___
17. Does security fit into the organization of the school?	___	___
18. Do students actively get involved in security efforts?	___	___
Do you include students on advisory safety boards?	___	___
19. Do parents actively get involved in security efforts?	___	___
20. Is there a working relationship with local law enforcement?	___	___
Are they available when needed?	___	___
Do they apply the law consistently?	___	___
Are they friendly and accepted by the students?	___	___
Do they help and advise on vandalism prevention?	___	___
Do they monitor school facilities during school hours?	___	___
21. Is there a policy to involve the community in safety awareness?	___	___
Is it being implemented?	___	___
How?		
By whom?		
Are local residents encouraged to report suspicious activity to school officials or police?	___	___
Are there public/private partnerships with business in place where you can tap security materials and resources?	___	___
22. Is there a policy on bullying?	___	___

Figure 2.3. Building Security Assessment Checklist *(continued)*

(continued)

Parts of the Planning Process 15

	Yes	No
23. Is there an open door policy that encourages students to report crime and violence?	___	___
Is this a policy that allows anonymity?	___	___
Is this policy supported?	___	___
Is this policy achieving its goals?	___	___
24. Is there a safety awareness policy?	___	___
Is it encouraged?	___	___
How?		
By whom?		
Do you put posters up to tell students?	___	___
25. Is there a policy to detect and control gang activity?	___	___
26. Is there a policy to investigate the background of volunteers working in the school?	___	___
Is this policy *rigorously* enforced?	___	___
By whom?		
27. Do you have policies and guidelines governing security and crowd control at special events?	___	___
Who is in charge?		

Existing security system

	Yes	No
28. Have there been any security problems in the past?	___	___
Are there prevention strategies in place to deal with them?	___	___
29. Do you know when and where the greatest number of crime and violence incidents occur on your campus?	___	___
30. Are valuable items of property identified?	___	___
31. Are high-target areas (such as the shop, administrative offices) sufficiently secured?	___	___
32. Is there an existing alarm system?	___	___
How is it activated?		
Is it self-resetting?	___	___
Who monitors it?		
Who maintains it?		
Who responds to it?		
How much does it cost per year?		
Is the system centrally located?	___	___
Is it local?	___	___
Is it a police alarm?	___	___
Do you have intrusion-detection equipment?	___	___
Have you consulted with an expert?	___	___
Is there a key control system?	___	___
Are high-target areas properly secured?	___	___
Is there a procedure for consistent maintenance and testing of the system (at least every 6 months)?	___	___

Figure 2.3. Building Security Assessment Checklist *(continued)*

(continued)

	Yes	No
Are the number of false alarms kept down to below two for any 6-month period?	___	___
Can selected areas of the school be "zoned" by an alarm system that will indicate which area is being entered by the intruder?	___	___
33. Do you have a policy as to alarm response and does everyone involved clearly understand his or her responsibilities?	___	___
34. Are suitable procedures established for response and turning on and off the alarm system?	___	___
35. Is there a two-way communication system between the classroom/office/principal? If not, why? Has the technology been investigated, and are the funds available?	___	___
36. Is there a system to communicate between the playground and the office?	___	___
37. Are parking lots monitored? Is there proper visibility of parking areas?	___ ___	___ ___
38. Is there a system to monitor the halls and restrooms? Is there supervision in hallways, corridors, and other places for students to congregate between classes, at lunch, and before and after school?	___ ___	___ ___
39. Is there a system for monitoring exits at the beginning and end of the school day?	___	___
40. Is there a system for monitoring the playground areas by parents, personnel, and law enforcement during recess?	___	___
41. Is there a system (e.g., drug-sniffing dogs) available to detect drugs, weapons, and violent behavior?	___	___
42. Are there regular drug detection inspections?	___	___
43. Are there metal detectors for weapons?	___	___

Target hardware/perimeter

	Yes	No
44. Does your local police department/fire department have a blueprint of your school building and perimeter?	___	___
45. Have local police or security inspected the school for security problems?	___	___
46. Is the school designed (landscaping, fencing, parking, and exterior lighting) with crime prevention in mind?	___	___
47. Is the school designed with vandal-resistant walls? Do the texture, color, and so on act to deter vandal activity?	___ ___	___ ___
48. Are signs properly designed for crime prevention (e.g., can't be pulled up easily)?	___	___

Figure 2.3. Building Security Assessment Checklist *(continued)*

(continued)

Parts of the Planning Process 17

	Yes	No

49. Are signs properly posted as to rules and enforcement? ___ ___
50. Is there proper fencing around adjacent areas and target areas? ___ ___
51. Are gates properly secured with working locks? ___ ___
52. Is the perimeter free of gravel or rocks? ___ ___
53. If there is exterior lighting, is it properly directed? ___ ___
    Is there proper intensity? ___ ___
    Are target areas well lighted? ___ ___
    Are there shadows? ___ ___
    Is there a light/no-light policy for after-school hours? ___ ___
    Are there break-resistant lenses on exterior lights? ___ ___
54. Are all grips, window ledges, roof access, and other equipment that could be used for climbing properly secured? ___ ___
55. Are all items removed from the building area that could be used to (a) break in or (b) stand and climb on? ___ ___
56. Are trash cans securely anchored? ___ ___
57. Do garbage Dumpsters or drain pipes provide access to the roof? ___ ___

Target hardware/exterior

58. Are all doors locked, except front entrance, after school starts? ___ ___
    Are outside handles removed from doors used primarily as exits? ___ ___
    Has the latest technology been investigated for safer doors? ___ ___
    Are doors equipped with security locks in mind? ___ ___
    Are locks maintained regularly and changed when necessary? ___ ___
    Are door frames pry-proof? ___ ___
    Are doors constructed properly? ___ ___
    Can any door locks be reached by breaking out glass? ___ ___
59. Are first-floor windows nonexistent or properly secured? ___ ___
60. Is broken glass replaced with Plexiglas or other break-resistant material? ___ ___
61. Are school facilities kept neat and in good repair? ___ ___
62. Is someone made responsible for overall school security procedures? ___ ___
63. Are security checklists used by school employees? ___ ___
64. Are there specific persons designated to secure buildings following after-hours activity? ___ ___
65. Is evening and weekend use of school facilities encouraged? (This cuts down on vandalism.) ___ ___

Figure 2.3. Building Security Assessment Checklist *(continued)*

(continued)

	Yes	No
66. Do law enforcement personnel, parents, or students patrol the grounds after school hours?	___	___
67. Are school facilities sectioned off to limit access by evening users?	___	___
68. Is after-hours use of playground facilities consistently and closely monitored?	___	___
69. Are protective screens or window guards used?	___	___
Target hardware/interior		
70. Is school property permanently and distinctly marked?	___	___
71. Has an inventory been made recently of school property?	___	___
72. Are school files locked in vandal-proof containers?	___	___
73. Are valuable items that thieves can easily fence (such as typewriters, calculators, computers) properly locked up or secured when not in use?	___	___
74. Is all money removed from cash registers?	___	___
75. Are cabinets properly secured?	___	___
76. Do teachers with windowless classrooms have flashlights?	___	___
77. If the utility power fails, is there a back-up power system and do teachers have flashlights to back up a total power failure?	___	___

Figure 2.3. Building Security Assessment Checklist *(continued)*

Step 5: Identify Current and Proposed Safety Features

locations, some checklist items may be more appropriate than others. Use the checklist to create one of your own.

As part of your planning process, it is important to develop a safety model that identifies programs, resources, and components that are already in place. If this type of model does not exist, your district could be viewed as liable in certain crisis situations. Remember, the district needs to do what is reasonable to prevent criminal or dangerous situations from happening. With a plan implemented, the district can show that it has reasonably identified and implemented a proactive program to minimize dangerous or traumatic crisis situations. Figure 2.4 is an example of the USA School District's development of this model.

The district should construct a diagram of all available security and safety elements that are actively implemented. Each school can identify an appropriate level of planning that addresses the predominant level of risk of harm in the school environment. Figure 2.4, a school safety and crisis management planning model, includes the dimensions of student and staff personal safety, security and school social environment, and security and school physical environment.

Parts of the Planning Process

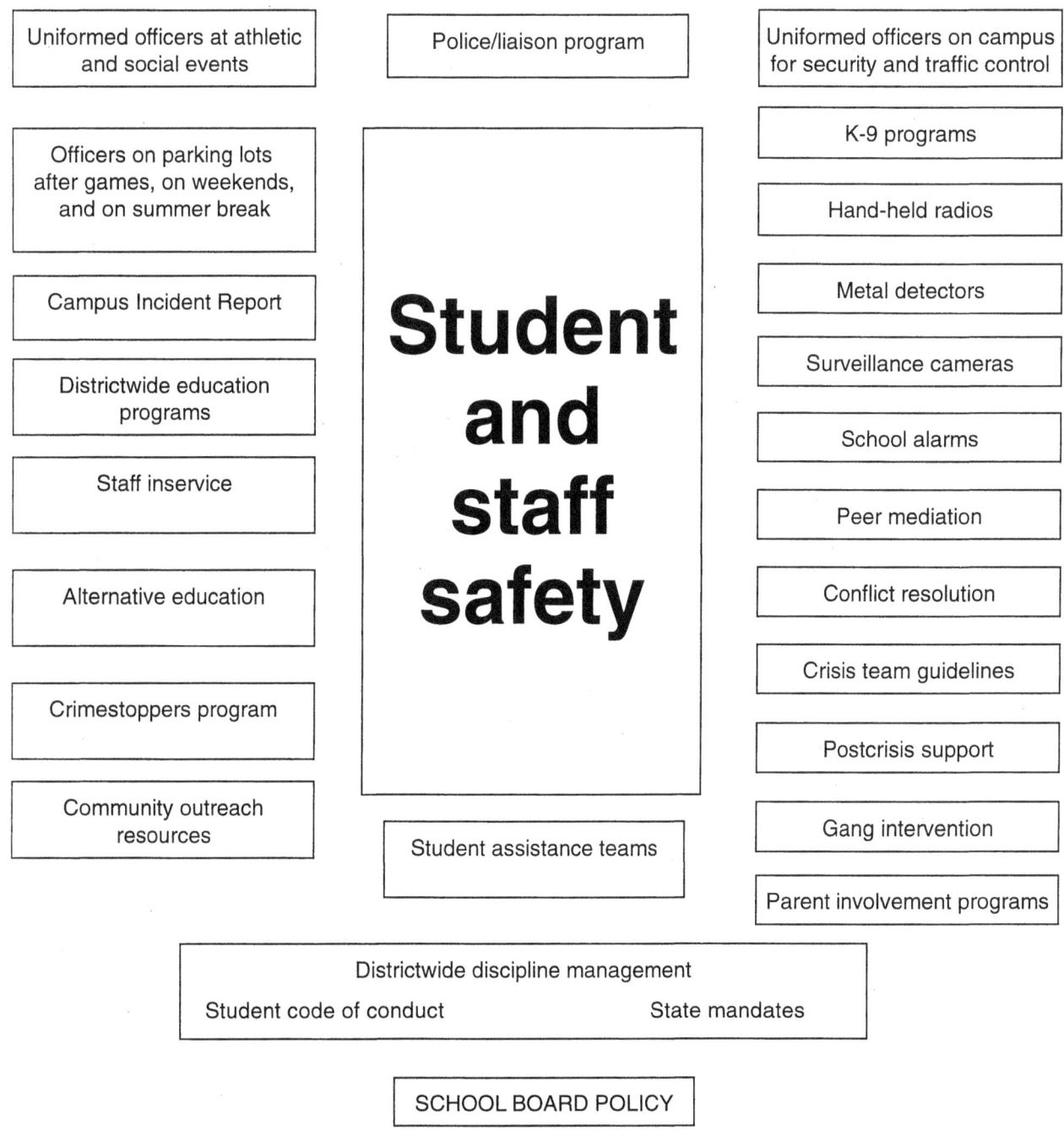

Figure 2.4. USA School District Safety and Crisis Management Planning Model

There are two key factors to the success of this type of planning. First, it assumes that there will be a continuous process of reevaluation, adjustment, modification, and improvement of conditions in the school environment. This planning process by the district monitors all of the school climate and safety dimensions previously listed to identify areas of critical need. It precludes immediate responses to all safety concerns,

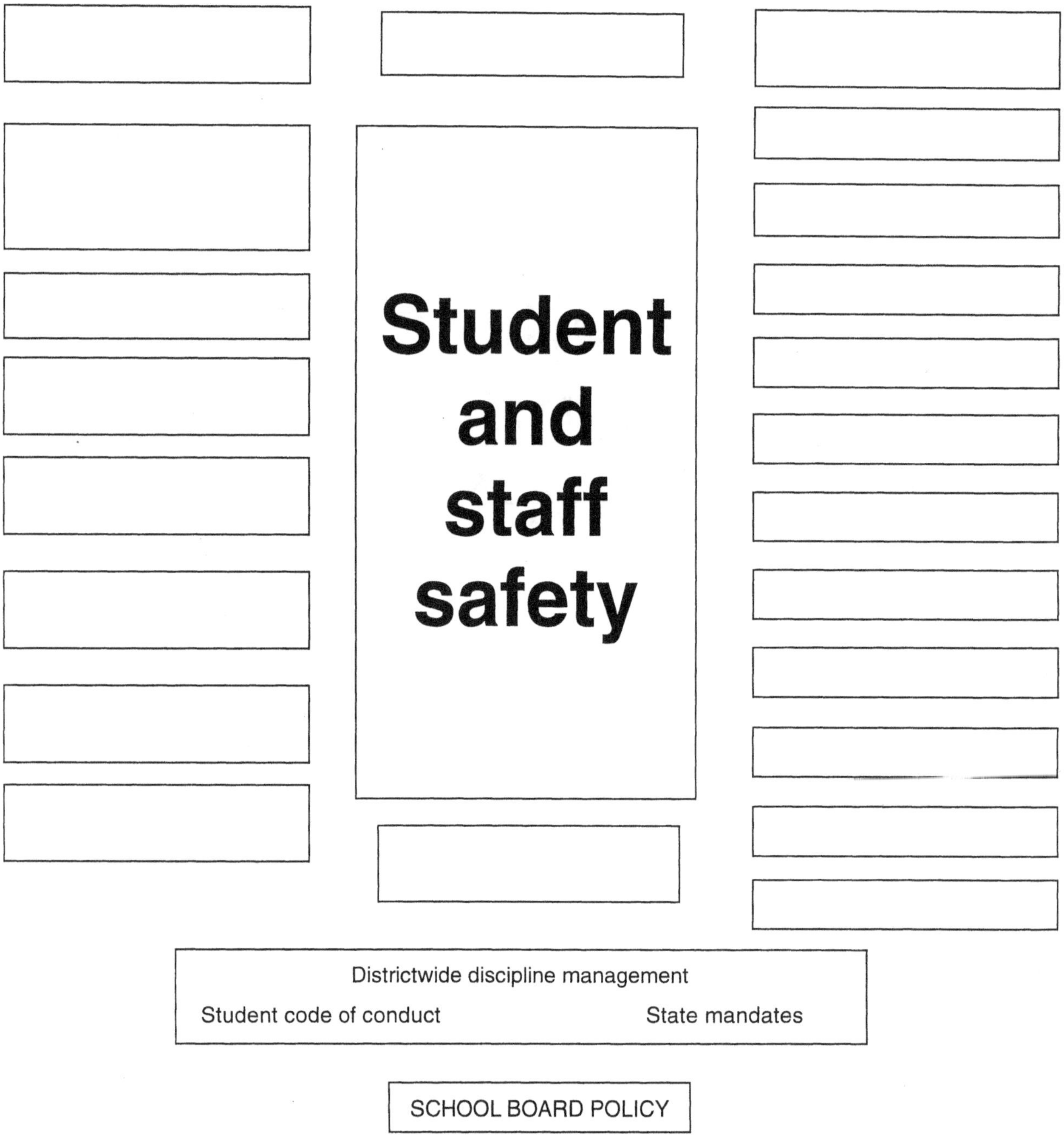

Student and staff safety

Districtwide discipline management	
Student code of conduct	State mandates

SCHOOL BOARD POLICY

Figure 2.5. Blank Safety and Crisis Management Planning Model

but those requiring immediate response are fully monitored. Figure 2.5 is provided as a blank model so that you can fill in your district's current procedures and programs. Ideally, this model could be developed by the district task force team and then presented to the school safety and crisis management team to assist it with identifying the most appropriate components.

Second, school safety and crisis management planning is systematic. Careful efforts are made to engage in "pre-action" stages of the planning process by building a consensus for the need to integrate safety and crisis management planning with other school improvement efforts. A "vision" of the development of principles to guide the planning process should be formalized before specific safety and crisis concerns or plans of action can be discussed. When this strong foundation is developed, the districtwide task force engages in a process that includes assessment activities, selection of actions, and evaluation.

As mentioned before, building a districtwide safety and crisis management plan begins with formally developing a mission statement. This statement has a unifying result: Because everyone involved wants to achieve the same outcome, there is a strong desire for the group to stick together. The ability to imagine what the ideal safe school would look like, feel like, and sound like is crucial to creating guidelines for a successful safety and crisis management plan.

The advantage of viewing safety concerns as discrepancies between the way things are and the way one would like them to be is that this approach enables a group to share a common vision—a clear sense of the importance of a safety and crisis management plan successfully implemented. The mission identification process can begin by simply asking task force team members to share their hopes, wishes, and desires about making their schools safe. Where would attention be focused? What would really make a difference at our schools? What is the most important thing to do to improve our schools' safety and crisis management capability?

Once the districtwide task force has refined a shared vision of a safe school, it is important to reach out to the school community and seek the opinions of other teachers, staff, students, parents, and community members. Procedures to collect and interpret data are established to create order out of the numerous sources of information available. When gathering information in an efficient manner, the district can take a fresh and objective look at the school environment.

The act of seeking opinions sends the message that there is concern for the school community and commitment to do something positive about school safety and crisis management. Existing records, questionnaires, interviews, and observations are ways to gather data about schools' safety and crisis concerns. It is essential that multiple sources of data be used to increase the validity of the safety and crisis management plan.

Chapter Three

The Safety and Crisis Management Team

On a sunny Friday morning in mid-October, Principal Elizabeth Fischer was reflecting on how smoothly the school year was going. There were no disgruntled parents, staff members were working well together, and the students were behaving beyond all expectations. Suddenly, she heard two gunshots. She raced out of her office and down the hallway to where some teachers were standing. As she was running down the hall, she observed an adult male hurriedly leaving the building. As she approached the classroom, she observed that her second-grade teacher had been shot in the classroom in front of the class. The teacher's ex-husband was taken into custody a few hours later and charged with the shooting.

How are you going to handle this crisis?
Remember, it's too late to think about it after it happens.

Step 6: Identify, Designate, and Document the Safety and Crisis Management Team

A workable crisis management plan must be comprehensive. The task of creating one is the responsibility of the principal, and cannot and should not be delegated to anyone else. In the eyes of the community, the principal is in charge of the school. Many decisions that are made to prevent or respond to a tragedy cannot be delegated. The principal is the one person the community holds responsible for action taken and not taken. However, this does not mean that the principal works in isolation in developing or implementing a safety and crisis management plan or crisis team. Every school has many professionals on its staff possessing expertise in various fields. Selecting key people from the staff to serve on an in-house safety crisis team ensures that all aspects of school life will be addressed. Furthermore, any plan developed by this team should be reviewed by the central administration office. Figure 3.1 establishes some guidelines for developing a safety and crisis management team.

The Safety and Crisis Management Team   23

Sample guidelines, established by a districtwide task force for developing a safety and crisis management team for campus or building, would include the following information.

The building principal shall be responsible for forming a safety and crisis management team for his or her campus using the following district guidelines:

- Designate appropriate personnel to serve on the safety and crisis management team(s) with the understanding that additions or substitutions may be made depending on the nature of the problem.
- Formulate a building safety and crisis management plan based on board policy and district task force guidelines.
- Define the mission and vision for viable programs and training to examine safety concerns and crisis response.
- Designate a place that will become the crisis management team's headquarters, and make sure it is appropriately equipped and has enough telephones. (It should be off site for media, parents, etc.)
- At regular intervals, assemble the crisis management team to review the overall safety and crisis management plan and to go over each individual's responsibilities.
- Maintain a log of events and actions during a crisis.
- Designate the individual who is to provide information to the administration building and to the media in the event of a crisis.

Figure 3.1. Guidelines for Developing a Safety and Crisis Management Team

This approach also provides the entire staff an opportunity to air any feelings or fears they might have about how they should handle a crisis. Once secure in their understanding, staff members will generate the support needed to implement the plan fully. More important, this airing should take place before any actual crisis, thus ensuring that the entire staff will be ready with a definite and positive plan of action when a crisis does occur.

Creating the Team

In Chapter 2, faculty members, staff members, and others were identified as potential team members. At this point, further elaboration needs to be made so a basic understanding can be developed for actually creating a team. Remember, each team and plan may be unique; the following is a suggested list of individuals who should be considered for the team and the rationale for their membership. Depending on your situation and circumstance, others may also be appropriate for inclusion on the team.

The principal. The principal is the chief executive officer of the building and/or campus and carries responsibility for all decisions made and actions taken. This individual is responsible for all activities associated with the educational experiences and safety of the students. For most buildings, the "buck" stops at the principal's office, whether the principal wants it to or not.

The principal's assistant or designee. The principal's assistant or designee is usually the person who substitutes for the principal when he or she is absent. The principal's assistant must be someone who commands the same respect and authority as the principal. This person should also be someone the principal trusts to make decisions similar to his or her own. Should a crisis occur during the principal's absence, this person must assume responsibility and set up a plan with which the principal can comfortably continue on return to the building.

A guidance counselor. A guidance counselor assigned to your school should be trained in children's reactions to crisis, emotional stages of grief, and group dynamics. This individual, or representatives of the Guidance Department, has access to an abundance of student information and is well connected with outside agencies that service the student population. The function of the guidance counselor or Guidance Department is to serve the students in a number of ways. During crisis situations, the Guidance Department becomes a key figure when working with students and parents. The individual or group of individuals should never be overlooked when it comes to identifying resources in anticipation of crisis situations. There are very few crisis situations where the Guidance Department will not play a significant role with students, parents, staff, and community.

Faculty members. The teaching staff should be represented by two or three individuals. These individuals should have the respect of co-workers and students alike and should know the climate of the school. These teachers need to be specially selected for membership to the team. Such considerations should be based on the teachers' location in the building, ability to remain calm under pressure, to exhibit clear thinking, follow through when given a task, and be comfortable talking about death and tragedy as well as being respected among their peers. These teachers must have leadership capabilities because their work on the team will be imperative to the success of dealing with the crisis.

A security/liaison officer. Smaller school districts and buildings may not have a need for a security/liaison officer; however, you may want to include such a person as a team member. If one is assigned to your school, he or she should be on the crisis team. Should a crisis involve an act of violence, your first response must be to provide for the safety of everyone in the building. For obvious reasons, this individual brings a wealth of resources and knowledge to the team. The contacts he or she has with the student body and the community will be a tremendous asset during times of crisis, and access to other community resources and agencies could prove to be a lifesaver in many school-related crisis situations. This individual would be familiar with the school campus and could provide vital information that could help protect the students and the staff.

Outside agency representative(s). Examples of these organizations are educational support services such as Iowa AEAs, New York BOCES, and Minnesota ECSUs, which provide services such as social workers and psychologists to local districts. Other community agencies should not be overlooked for providing representatives to the team. Remember, a crisis is no time to be thinking about what resources are available and asking yourself, "Could they help?" Plan for the day when it *is* going to happen.

A school nurse. As a member of the team, this individual will provide information as to the need for medical expertise, will have access to first aid equipment, medical records of students, and information concerning community resources associated with medical treatment. When a crisis hits and your students and/or staff are in need of medical attention, it is too late to think about fundamentals like supplies, records, and additional medical help. The school nurse has the information that is needed and becomes a valuable asset for first-response medical attention.

A clerical representative. School buildings have a valuable clerical staff that assists teachers, administrators, and students in all aspects of the educational experience. A representative should be a part of the safety and crisis management team. During a time of crisis, everyone wants to know what is happening or what is going to happen. Parents will be making frantic calls to the school wondering about their children, the news media will call, community agencies will call, and local authorities will want to get in touch with the building administration. These are just a few examples of the types of calls that need to be addressed when a crisis hits. The building principal is not the person to be answering the telephone during this time. He or she will probably be making numerous decisions, some of which could result in life-or-death situations. Competent clerical help who are trained to respond in a calm and appropriate way are needed to give confidence that the situation is under control.

A custodial representative/building engineer. Just as important as clerical staff members are in times of crisis, custodial staff members also play a very important role during times of crisis. These individuals have building floorplans and keys for everything. They know more about the building than any other individual, including the principal. They have access to supplies that may be needed during the crisis situation. These individuals have a wealth of knowledge concerning the intricacies of the building and where everything is located, not only in the building but in outbuildings or secondary buildings that may be on your campus. They can get to places where you, the administrator, never knew existed.

Others. Other staff and community members should be added to the crisis team as specific plans are developed and implemented. Depending on the plan that your school put together, individuals from Food Service should be consulted. Their input could be significant. Also, volunteers should not be overlooked. From time to time, parent and community volunteers may be asked to lend support, and it is nice to have a representative to organize a pool of individuals for help.

Figure 3.2 is a sample form that could be used by the safety and crisis management team to provide valuable information on quick notice. This form will identify team members, their location for communication purposes, and their responsibilities. One copy should be kept on file in the school building, and a second copy should be kept on file in the district office.

Preferred Personality Characteristics of Crisis Team Members

As you, the principal, look to your staff and community for membership on your team, there are some personal characteristics that you should look for in potential members. Good team members have

- A broad perspective on life
- An ability to anticipate multiple consequences
- A willingness to challenge an idea and then work cooperatively toward a solution
- An ability to think under stress
- Flexibility
- Familiarity with nuances of the school, its students, and its community

Crucial characteristics are the ability to anticipate multiple consequences and the ability to think under stress. An individual who is insightful and has the forethought to be able to identify numerous consequences to a particular action will be an invaluable team member in the development of a prevention program as well as during the time of a crisis. Similarly, the team member who can think under stress is extremely valuable when clear minds need to prevail. Committing "fatal errors" is a dangerous path to follow. A better end result will be possible when a proactive and preplanned process is undertaken. During times of crisis and high-stress activities, fatal action errors have a tendency to

Effective date: _____

Campus: _____

Chairperson: _____

Name: _____

Title: _____

Home address: _____

Telephone/home: _____

Telephone/office: _____

Responsibilities during crisis: _____

_____

Committee members: (include building principal or designee, guidance counselor, faculty member, security officer, school psychologist, site operations specialists, secretary, bus driver, nurse)

Name: _____

Title: _____

Home address: _____

Telephone/home: _____

Telephone/office: _____

Responsibilities during crisis: _____

_____

Name: _____

Title: _____

Home address: _____

Telephone/home: _____

Telephone/office: _____

Responsibilities during crisis: _____

_____

Figure 3.2. Sample Safety and Crisis Management Team Information Form

happen. Proper planning will not eliminated poor judgment or libelous actions, but it will minimize major problems associated with a difficult situation.

Guidelines for the Safety and Crisis Management Team

When a crisis hits, be prepared for an extremely intense day. Obviously, you will not be able to anticipate any specific day that will turn into a crisis, but when one comes your way, the adrenaline will start flowing and it may flow for an extended period of time. Remember continually that you are making and will make a difference. Students will look to you for help.

As a member of the safety and crisis management team, be prepared to meet on short notice. Crisis situations have no timetable and do not give forewarning. Part of the plan must deal with team members, if necessary, to be relieved from teaching duties on very short notice. This can be planned for in advance.

General safety and crisis management procedures need to be available for quick review. This means that specific plans need to be implemented and not developed during a crisis situation. As a team, you will probably not have the time to do a great deal of planning but will generally be placed into a reactive mode.

The safety and crisis management team shall assist the principal with a number of duties that will need to be taken care of immediately following the crisis, such as writing a memo to be presented to the student body; just being available for students, staff, or parents who may be in need of assistance; calling staff members and informing them of an upcoming meeting; assisting the principal when there is a staff meeting; and assisting with a meeting of concerned parents, if such a meeting is deemed appropriate. Figure 3.3 lists some additional guidelines for crisis team members. Many of the guidelines are situational and need to be discussed as appropriate given different school organizational environments.

As part of the crisis management plan, a list of crisis team members with home telephone numbers, pager numbers, and building location should be identified. Building diagram/floorplan with zoned areas of building responsibility should be identified. The plan should identify any staging or alternative evacuation site(s). Each staff member should know where the staff will meet (site/location) if communication is cut off. For example, if power has totally been cut off and there is no communication in the building, staff members need to know where to go to get information and/or help. The plan needs to identify the source of official information (radio, newspaper, television station, etc.). This can be done ahead of time so the staff can with confidence be able to detect truth from rumor as information becomes available.

Other Considerations

Other major considerations of the building safety and crisis management team would be to communicate only the facts of the critical situ-

The Safety and Crisis Management Team

On the day of the crisis, be prepared for an extremely intense day. You will make a difference. Students will look to you for help.

1. You must be able to meet on short notice.
2. You should be able to have quick access to the procedures.
3. Be prepared to help write memo to be presented to students.
4. When talking about the situation, stick to the facts.
5. Be available for students, staff, or parents in need of assistance.
6. Call other staff members and inform them of the upcoming meeting.
7. Meet with staff.
8. One member of the crisis team may follow a student's schedule.
9. Make formal acknowledgement of the loss/crisis to parents.
10. Identify students at risk and contact parents.
11. Set up follow-up services for students.
12. Back-up support team will be available as long as needed.
13. The safety and crisis management team may wish to conduct a meeting of concerned parents.
14. Make certain that the crisis plan is prominently displayed in key areas of the building. Every employee should have a copy of the plan.
15. Designate a command post in your building. Appoint a person to stay at the telephone and radio.
16. Assign a written chain of command in your building.
17. Ensure that first aid equipment/infectious disease supplies are available in designated areas.
18. The secretary will secure all records and office valuables in a safe place.
19. Confirm that the roll and count of students are received at the command post.
20. Media and other requests for information should be referred to the building principal or district public relations specialist.

Figure 3.3. General Guidelines for the Safety and Crisis Management Team

ation. Figure 3.4 gives an example of factual information that is needed so that correct information can be presented as fact. As a member of the team, you will be perceived as knowledgeable about all of the facts of the crisis. Giving information that has not been verified may cause additional harm or trauma to individuals receiving your information. When talking about the situation, stick to the facts. When confronted with the media and/or other requests for information, refer these individuals to the building principal or district public relations specialist.

To answer media/telephone inquiries during a crisis, know the facts:

1. What happened? _____
   _____
   _____

2. When did the event occur? _____

3. Where did the event occur? _____

4. Who is involved? (*Caution: Do not give out names of deceased or injured until the family has been notified.*) _____
   _____

5. Other traumas: _____

6. Is there any apparent reason why this crisis occurred? _____
   _____
   _____

7. What is being done by school and emergency personnel? _____
   _____
   _____

8. If students are to be released or excused to attend a funeral, what is the correct procedure? _____
   _____
   _____

9. Will school be closed or classes held in another facility? If so, where?
   _____

10. Are any meetings planned for parents or community? When? Where?
    _____
    _____
    _____

11. What is being planned to help families affected by the crisis?
    _____
    _____
    _____

Figure 3.4. Crisis Fact Sheet

Chapter Four

The Plan

Principal Teresa Coenen, a first-year principal, was reflecting about the development of a crisis management plan for her building one late afternoon after everyone had left for the day. She was quite concerned that there was no board policy or procedure if there was a crisis situation. Mrs. Coenen had no idea what was involved in the development of a plan, but she did know that she wanted her faculty and staff involved in the development of a plan. She thought to herself, where do I start and how do the faculty and I accomplish such a project?

Do you find yourself in a similar situation?
Where do I start? Whom do I involve?
Is there a model that can be modified or implemented?

Development of an Action Plan and a "Table of Contents" for the Building Document

These two steps are closely associated with one another. Administrators will need to become involved with how the plan will be organized, objectives and goals of such a plan, what type of staff training will need to take place, initiating the plan, making the staff and community aware of the plan as well as promoting the plan, plan evaluation, and finally, plan maintenance and growth.

> **Goal 1:** Provide a safe environment for learning
>
> **Goal 2:** Prevent crime and violence on campus
>
> **Goal 3:** Train students and staff in crime prevention and personal safety programs and techniques
>
> **Goal 4:** Involve the community

Figure 4.1. Goals for Safety

Step 7: Set Goals and Guidelines for Developing Building-Level Plans

The safety and crisis management plan should be based on board policy and district guidelines. The plan is a framework for duties related to securing a safe school: the preparation for and the prevention, management, and resolution of a crisis. Examples of some of these goals are given in Figure 4.1.

Along with developing goals for a safe environment, there is a need to develop goals for crisis and postcrisis management. These goals will serve as the foundation and beginning of developing a site-based crisis management plan. Figure 4.2 includes examples that could be used as a basis for the crisis management part of the total safety and crisis management plan.

Crisis Information Dissemination Process

When a crisis occurs, an administrator needs to react to the situation. One of the most important first steps is to provide information to a number of people and/or organizations or agencies. Figure 4.3 is an example of a dissemination process that identifies the appropriate and necessary agencies and individuals. This information-reporting process will not change depending on the crisis; however, there may be some telephone calls that may be inappropriate, depending on the specific crisis. An example of this is that the local police department may not need to be called if the crisis happened over a weekend and is a student crisis where the school is reacting to an emotional situation. On the other hand, it may be very appropriate if the situation is similar to the crisis presented at

> **Goal 1:** Contain a crisis
>
> **Goal 2:** Prevent injury to students, staff, and faculty
>
> **Goal 3:** Care for the injured and notify parents
>
> **Goal 4:** Prevent damage to school property
>
> **Goal 5:** Provide information to news media and the public
>
> **Goal 6:** Return school to normal functioning order

Figure 4.2. Goals for Crisis and Postcrisis Management

The following route of notification must be done 7 days per week, 24 hours per day.

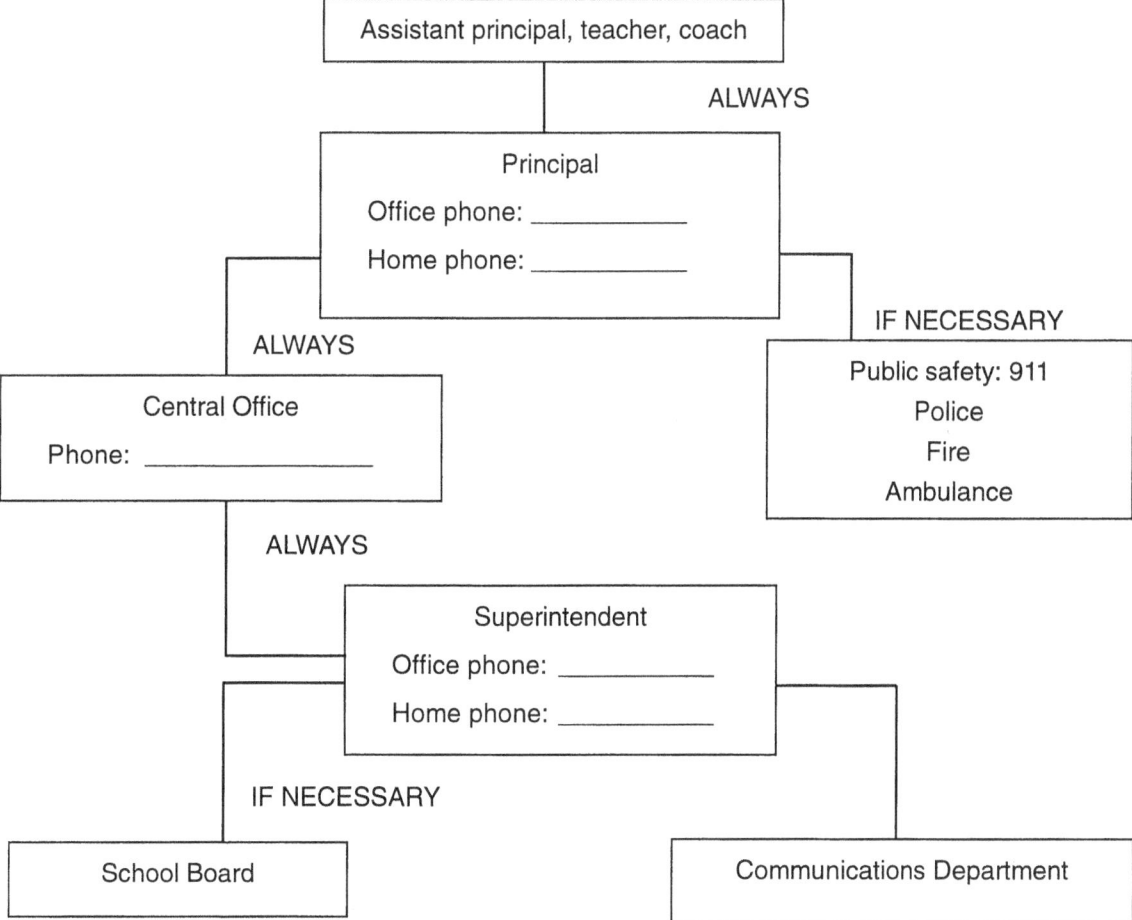

Figure 4.3. Crisis Information Dissemination Flowchart

the beginning of the chapter. If, for example, a tornado hits your building and communication has not been disrupted, it is very appropriate that local authorities be notified for assistance.

One suggestion that each school or campus needs to evaluate is the need for a cellular telephone in times of emergency. When the conventional telephone service is no longer available, the use of a cellular telephone may be a lifesaver.

Step 8: Develop a "Table of Contents" for the Building Safety and Crisis Management Plan

In building your plan, it is wise to develop a table of contents first before proceeding with the actual written document. This will minimize the chances of mistakenly leaving out a valuable piece of the plan. Figure 4.4 will help you in identifying your plan components and will set your committee in motion to gather useful information.

I. Introduction
Introduction
Developing a safety and crisis management team
Statement of safety and crisis management director's responsibility

II. Communications
Campus Incident Report
Communication chain during major crisis
Crisis Resource List
Emergency numbers
Media contacts
Safety poster program

III. Building-Level Crisis
Accidents and medical emergencies
    Serious injury or death
Accidents to and from school
Alcohol, suspicion or possession of
Alternate school location
Bomb threats, telephone threats, and other disruptive demonstrations
    Threat Call Checklist
Breaking up fights
Child abuse (suspected) reporting procedures
    Report of Suspected Child Abuse or Neglect
Child kidnapping
Children left at school
Communicating with the media
Confidentiality
Controlled substance, suspicion or possession of
Custody laws affecting the school
Drug screening
Drug abuse resources
Employee emergency information
Explosion or fire
Gang or cult activity
Gas leaks
Hazardous materials spill
Hostage situation
Injuries, illness—How to handle when persons on the enrollment card
    cannot be reached
Local building communication chain
Loitering in or around building
Missing or runaway child
Parent procedures for picking up children in a crisis
Person(s) in charge when the principal is away
Psychological services
Security breach/vandalism
Stranger in the building
Suicide threats and attempts
    Suicide Questionnaire
    Contract
    Bibliography of resources

Figure 4.4. Example of Table of Contents Components

The Plan

　　Tornado, hurricane, earthquake, and other disaster plans
　　Weapons on campus

IV. Districtwide Crisis
　　Bus accidents with serious injury and/or fatality
　　Bus and auto accidents on trips away from district
　　Bus failure
　　Communicating with the media
　　Flood disaster planning
　　Hurricane disaster planning
　　Power failure or lines down in area
　　Tornado disaster planning
　　Weather closings and announcements

V. Prevention and Safety Strategies
　　Building security
　　Classroom safety issues
　　Conflict resolution
　　Community outreach programs
　　Crowd control
　　D.A.R.E.
　　Gang awareness
　　Law enforcement linkage
　　Peer mediation
　　Safety procedures to and from school events
　　Surveillance techniques
　　Violence prevention curriculum
　　Zero tolerance

VI. Forms
　　Campus crisis management team
　　Campus Incident Report
　　Crisis Resource List
　　Crisis Fact Sheet
　　Local building communication chain
　　Notification of emergency conference
　　Persons in charge when the principal is away
　　Principal's Crisis Management Checklist
　　Report of Suspected Child Abuse or Neglect
　　Suicide Questionnaire
　　Threat Call Checklist

Figure 4.4. Example of Table of Contents Components *(continued)*

Step 9: Develop a Safety and Crisis Management Plan

The building principal shall be responsible for initiating a safety and crisis management plan for his or her building or campus. A visionary action plan needs to be developed that will assist the principal (see Figures 4.5 and 4.6). As principal, you should designate appropriate personnel to serve on the team with the understanding that additions or substitutions may be made depending on the nature of the problem. Remember, your team must be based on board policy and district task force guidelines. Figure 4.6 can assist you in identifying major components of a

Individual Form

Personal characteristics of students and staff
　　The traits that students, teachers, administrators, and other personnel bring to the school (ethnic/cultural diversity, experiences)

　　My prevention/intervention goals:

Social environment of the school
　　The organizational and interpersonal processes that occur in and around the school (structure, procedures, organization)

　　My/our prevention/intervention goals:

Physical environment of the school
　　The physical condition in which education takes place (location, buildings, classrooms)

　　My/our prevention/intervention goals:

Cultural characteristics of the school
　　The general atmosphere or spirit of the school (norms, beliefs, values)
　　My/our prevention/intervention goals:

Group Consensus Form

Our shared vision for a safe school and overall goals
Our shared vision:

Our goals:
　　1.
　　2.
　　3.
　　4.
　　5.
　　6.

Comments:

Data Summary

Areas of pride and strength

Areas of concern and need

Comments

Figure 4.5. Creating a Vision

Planning and Organizing

Identify members and form building safety and crisis management team
Use incidents reports to assess prevention and early intervention needs
Use building survey checklist to assess strengths and weaknesses
Review district guidelines. Amend or add as appropriate to encompass issues/needs of building
Using model, formulate a summary of how to address safety needs and improve on components already in place
Research new technology and make recommendations
Identify how the safety and crisis management plan can link with law enforcement
Set guidelines for involvement of students, parents, community outreach
Begin to consider the various funding possibilities, and coordinate the proposal with district budget timeline
Solicit input and feedback from other principals and other appropriate staff, administrators, and parents

Safety and Crisis Management Plan Development

Develop overall plan goals
Identify training needs and resources, and establish a training plan for the safety and crisis management team
Define student support services component
Define the curriculum and classroom support component with goals
Define the parent and community outreach component with goals and services
Define the linkage with law enforcement with goals and services component
Develop recommendations for staffing and plan coordination
Decide whether to pilot the plan or any component or to proceed with districtwide implementation
Develop a budget and funding proposal. Check the district budget process timeline
Identify to formulate community outreach collaboration and partnership strategies
Develop plan proposal for the district that includes:
   Description of safety and crisis management plan framework including goals and services
   Linkage to all appropriate district goals, priorities, initiatives
   Staffing and coordination needs
   Budget and funding proposals
   Timeline for program staff training and implementation
Identify all possible plan challenges and concerns, and begin to formulate positive responses
Solicit feedback from other principals and appropriate administrators on the plan proposal prior to presenting it to the district/board of education

Figure 4.6. Developing an Action Plan

(continued)

building or campus plan. Each of these components should be well thought-out and planned for as the document is prepared to be operationalized.

Training Staff

Begin initial program staff training.
Complete a safety and crisis management plan handbook.
Arrange ongoing training inservice, and plan support meetings.

Plan Initiation

Secure basic program equipment and supplies.
Secure plan content materials.

Plan Awareness and Promotion

Staff	Develop and conduct school staff inservice.
	Develop a staff handbook.
	Conduct a staff needs assessment.
	Consider developing a staff newsletter and other staff update strategies.
	Check on the availability of inservice for psychologists, social workers, law enforcement, and other pertinent special education staff.
Students	Decide on ways the students will access the plan.
	Plan and conduct classroom visits to introduce the plan to students.
	Consider placing a student on the safety and crisis management team.
	Consider safety and crisis management team teaching with counselors, security officers, and so on as a way to bring the plan to the students.
	Devise a poster awareness program for safety.
Parents	Prepare and send an introductory letter to parents from the principal.
	Develop and print a plan brochure for parents.
	Design a logo to symbolize any information about the plan.
	Develop and distribute parent needs assessments; compile results and do parent outreach activities.
	Plan a parent information night or PTA meeting session.
	Plan a regular column for the school newsletter.
Community groups	Consider a community education series to various outreach groups or agencies.
	Develop a presentation for the Neighborhood Watch or other possible collaboration activities.
	Develop public-private partnerships with local businesses to provide resources, equipment and security materials, ideas, and so on.
	Contact local newspapers and local cable TV to publicize positive preventive activities instead of waiting for crisis coverage.
	Consider presenting a program overview at state or national conferences. Feedback will be beneficial to growth.

Figure 4.6. Developing an Action Plan *(continued)*

Plan Evaluation

Determine roles and responsibilities for program evaluation
Develop instrumentation and timeline
Analyze data at designated intervals and adjust the plan accordingly
Conduct end of the analysis and prepare reports on the results for board, administrators, staff, parents, and community

Plan Maintenance and Growth

Consider how to prevent the deterioration of the plan
Develop a system for continued and increased plan awareness
Develop goals for continued and increased plan awareness
Develop goals to specifically broaden plan involvement as well as ongoing training
Consider ways to celebrate and revitalize the people and the plan

Figure 4.6. Developing an Action Plan *(continued)*

As part of your building plan, you must emphasize the mission and vision for such a team to help build ownership among and within the faculty and staff of your building or campus. Emphasize the need for training and staff development. This will promote ownership and raise the level of seriousness to the project.

The first steps to developing an effective school safety and crisis management plan should be to provide each staff member with a copy of the district's emergency procedures manual. Every school district should have such a manual, and every teacher should have access to such a manual. Every staff member in your building should know who is on the team and their responsibilities. Along with the active members on the team, alternate members should be identified. These individuals would represent support resources during crisis situations.

An excellent safety and crisis management plan will also include a designated place that will become the safety and crisis management team's headquarters. Make sure it is appropriately equipped and has enough telephones—plus a cellular telephone—to meet the challenge. The building administrator should be located in one place and not be wondering around the building or campus. Many decisions may need to be made on very short notice and sometimes on the spot by the administrator. It will facilitate the management plan if the administrator is readily accessible. Remember, that is why you have a crisis team: to assist you in the many events that are going to be happening all at once. Perception and planning are the important parts of the crisis management process.

The crisis management plan should include a list of crisis team members' names, home telephone numbers, pager numbers, and building locations. The building diagram/floorplan with zoned areas of building responsibility should be identified, and the plan should identify any staging or alternative evacuation site(s). Each staff member should know where to meet if communication is cut off and where to go to get information and/or help. The plan needs to identify the source of official information. This should be done ahead of time so the staff can be able to detect truth from rumor as information becomes available.

Standard Plans Should Provide for the Most Common Crisis Situations

When the plan is being developed, it should include the assignment of responsibilities as well as situation plans and procedures. The standard situation plans and procedures for all school building and campuses are as follows:

- Bomb threat management
- Fire drill evacuation plan with alternative escape plans
- Tornado, hurricane, or earthquake drill and structural safe area identified
- School evacuation plan for dangerous situations
- Reporting system for missing/unaccounted for, injured/safe students/personnel
- Unauthorized persons, intruders
- Alternative campus/building notification when P.A. is not practical
- Crime scene protection/weapon recovery
- Violent crime suppression
- Violence prevention drills for student safety
- Teacher room assignments and time periods

As part of every safety and crisis preparedness plan, the supplies identified in Figure 4.7 are recommended for emergency preparedness. Along with the supplies, their location within the building or campus should be identified. An inventory should be taken of these supplies annually to make sure they are available and in working order. *Do not wait until you need them to see if they work.*

Staff development is also part of developing a safety and crisis management plan to make sure that the plan can be activated and carried out in an efficient manner. This requires that individuals practice or conduct crisis drills. A crisis drill should provide an opportunity to practice your response, not to frighten everybody. The drill scenario should remain real enough to get the adrenaline flowing and to identify potential areas for improvement.

Drills involving firearms should not be conducted with students, unless very limited in scope and restricted to a controlled environment.

Flashlights with fresh batteries
Bullhorn (hand-held P.A.)
Weather alert radio
AM/FM battery-powered radio
Cellular telephone
Trauma bandages, first aid kit, and blankets
Triage tags (red, yellow, green, and black tags)
Rubber gloves, work gloves
List of emergency numbers:
  Emergency service providers
  Utilities companies, emergency and after-hours numbers
  District crisis team member list
Copy of district crisis plan
Master roll printout with telephone numbers and emergency numbers
Up-to-date building diagram or floorplan
Lightweight storage container for emergency supplies

Remember to identify where these supplies are located

Figure 4.7. Recommended Supplies for Safety and Crisis Management Team

Remember, overly dramatic drill scenarios may inspire real-life copycats.

At regular intervals, the safety and crisis management team leader (principal) should assemble the team to review the overall safety and crisis plan and to go over each individual's responsibilities.

What Should Your Plan Look Like in Regard to Student Attendance?

When an in-school crisis occurs, it is imperative that student supervision and accountability be maintained. This means that all students need to be accounted for and parents contacted when necessary to notify them of their child's absence or need of medical attention. A plan of student roll taking and reporting needs to be done with the utmost speed and efficiency. During a crisis and/or trauma situation, some students will want to leave the building or campus. Administrators, teachers, and staff must be aware of this possibility and maintain careful and accurate supervision of students. All students must be aware of the policy that no one leaves the building or campus without permission. Parents must be called when a student is discovered to be missing. This type of situation can handicap the administration and the safety and crisis management team and divert their attention to missing students who have left the building and/or campus without permission, complicating the crisis situation that has developed. It is imperative not only that a plan be in place but that staff development training be implemented so faculty and staff can become familiar with a very important procedure. The lives of students are the real concern of everyone in the building.

Outside Support Groups and Volunteers

The initial building safety and crisis management team needs to lend support for those services that are unique or special to a particular crisis. When outside support groups are needed to assist with the crisis situation and are not familiar with the facility locations or building environment, safety and crisis management team members can assist outside support team members to become familiar with the facility and environment.

Following the Crisis Response Checklist

When a crisis happens, the principal or a designated crisis team member needs to activate the Crisis Response Checklist. Figure 4.8 identifies items that need to be taken care of, probably in a very short time period. Remember, it takes a team to take care of a crisis situation. Crisis team members play a tremendously valuable role during the early stages of a crisis. Make sure your checklist is followed as designed in the planning stages.

Faculty and Staff Roles During a Crisis

The principal needs to be highly visible. Students and staff need to have confidence that the situation is under control, as much as possible, and they need to know that everything is being done to minimize problems and maximize a safe environment. The principal will usually be the person to address the media and contact the central administration and/or board of education. The principal sets the tone and direction of resolving the safety or crisis situation. The principal is also the person who activates and chairs the crisis team.

One of the first steps a principal takes is to activate his or her Crisis Resource List (see Figure 4.9). This immediately helps the administrator with valuable information on how to contact individuals who can assist in the crisis. This could also be done by the principal's designee, such as another crisis team member. The principal must also make sure that all the bases are covered. This requires a checklist so that all of the necessary procedures are completed.

The faculty play an important role during a crisis situation. Obviously, their main role is student safety. Teachers usually are the ones who announce to students and react to events in their class. Teachers

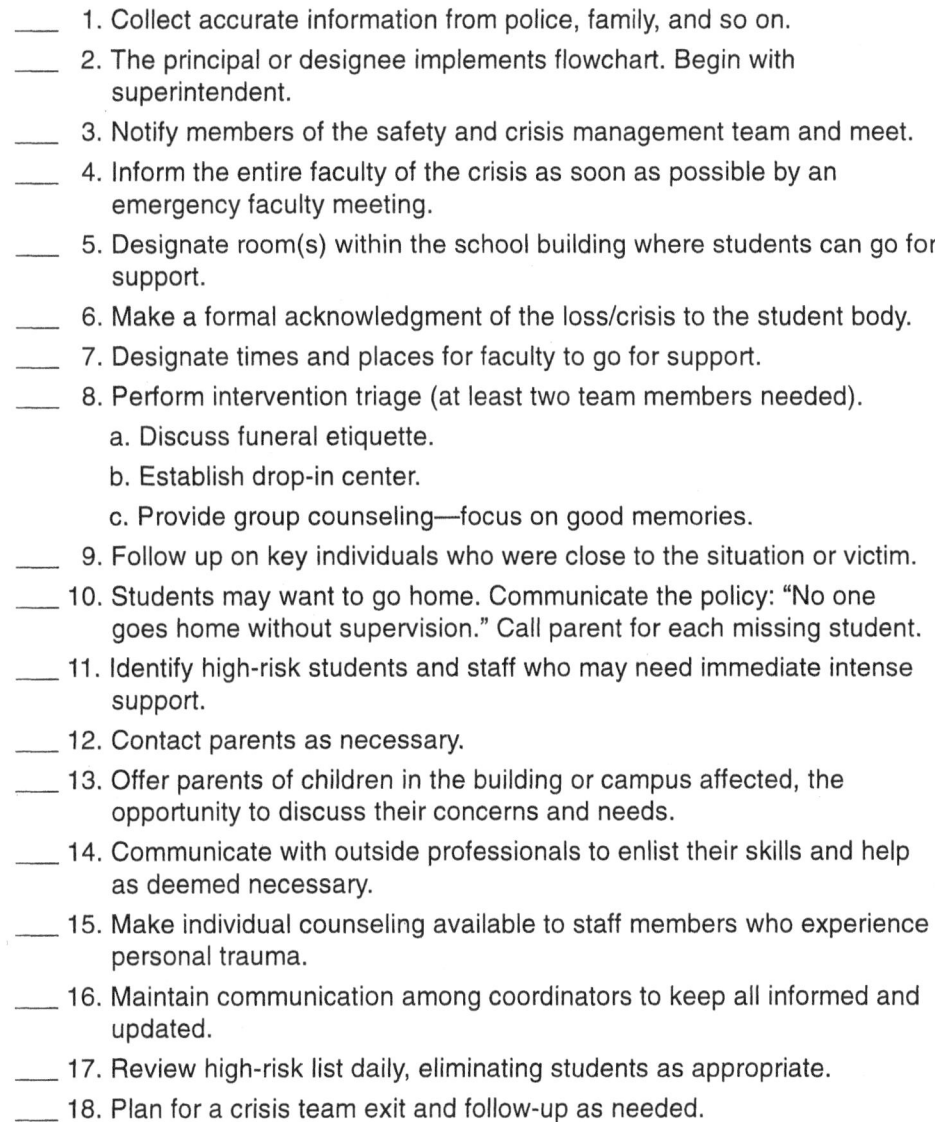

___ 1. Collect accurate information from police, family, and so on.
___ 2. The principal or designee implements flowchart. Begin with superintendent.
___ 3. Notify members of the safety and crisis management team and meet.
___ 4. Inform the entire faculty of the crisis as soon as possible by an emergency faculty meeting.
___ 5. Designate room(s) within the school building where students can go for support.
___ 6. Make a formal acknowledgment of the loss/crisis to the student body.
___ 7. Designate times and places for faculty to go for support.
___ 8. Perform intervention triage (at least two team members needed).
    a. Discuss funeral etiquette.
    b. Establish drop-in center.
    c. Provide group counseling—focus on good memories.
___ 9. Follow up on key individuals who were close to the situation or victim.
___ 10. Students may want to go home. Communicate the policy: "No one goes home without supervision." Call parent for each missing student.
___ 11. Identify high-risk students and staff who may need immediate intense support.
___ 12. Contact parents as necessary.
___ 13. Offer parents of children in the building or campus affected, the opportunity to discuss their concerns and needs.
___ 14. Communicate with outside professionals to enlist their skills and help as deemed necessary.
___ 15. Make individual counseling available to staff members who experience personal trauma.
___ 16. Maintain communication among coordinators to keep all informed and updated.
___ 17. Review high-risk list daily, eliminating students as appropriate.
___ 18. Plan for a crisis team exit and follow-up as needed.

Figure 4.8. Example of a Crisis Response Checklist

need to be trained to deal with many different situations and conditions regarding classroom management and control. The middle of a crisis is no time to start the reflection process about what to do. It is a time of reaction and knowing what to do. As mentioned previously, the safety of students should be the primary motive for a teacher's reactions. The teacher needs to identify students who are in need of counseling and medical attention. If the teacher is going to be in charge and supervise the students during a crisis situation, then the teacher needs to generate activities to reduce the effect of the traumatic situation. Structure on the part of the teacher is very important to the secure comfort and safety of students. Short assignments are preferred over longer ones, and all testing should be postponed until the crisis situation is over. Students will

Develop a list similar to this using the specific resources available in your community.

School board office — **Name and telephone number**
- Superintendent _____
- Student services director _____
- Crisis team _____
- Security officer _____

School support staff — **Name and telephone number**
- School psychologist _____
- School social worker _____
- School nurse _____
- School physician _____
- _____
- _____

Community agencies — **Location and telephone number**
- Youth crisis center _____
- Mental health clinic _____
- Suicide prevention center _____
- Hospice _____
- Police _____
- Rescue squad _____
- Victims assistance services _____
- Health and human service _____
- Rape crisis center _____
- Clergy _____
- _____
- _____
- _____

Parent volunteers — **Name and telephone number**
- _____
- _____
- _____
- _____

Figure 4.9. Crisis Resource List

Principal
  Remain highly visible
  Address media
  Contact school board
  Set tone and direction
  Chair crisis team

Counselor
  Provide counseling for students
  Plan logistics of counseling
  Coordinate all counseling activities
  Communicate with faculty
  Cancel scheduled activities
  Seek additional counseling support
  Contact feeder schools
  Seek additional secretarial support
  Provide information to parents

Faculty
  Announce events to students
  Lead class discussion
  Identify students in need of counseling
  Generate activities to reduce effect of trauma
  Structure and shorten assignments
  Postpone testing

Figure 4.10. Staff Roles During a Crisis

be perceiving the pressure of the crisis situation and do not need the added pressure of a test environment.

Support staff members in the building or on campus share a very important role during time of crisis. These individuals are the glue that holds the team together. They are the ones who know where supplies are located, have the blueprints of all parts of the building or campus, and can help in evacuation or medical help situations. They are utility people who can assist in a number of areas, and if trained can be a lifesaving support in dangerous situations. Figure 4.10 can be used as a checklist to help make your plan as complete as possible.

The Counselor or Counseling Department Roles During a Crisis

The counselor or Counseling Department has a number of things to do in a very short time. Counselors need to ready themselves to counsel students, depending on the crisis situation. Logistic plans involving counseling need to be readied and implemented. The coordination of the counseling effort and all activities need to be enacted and put into operation on a moment's notice. Communication with the faculty is vital from the

___ 1. Monitor students who are at risk for postcrisis trauma. Provide counseling.
___ 2. Determine parents or faculty needing counseling.
___ 3. Determine where/when follow-up counseling will take place.
___ 4. Determine if outside resources are needed or *wanted* by personnel.
___ 5. Debrief faculty and staff.
___ 6. Debrief safety and crisis management team.
___ 7. Evaluate actions taken.

Figure 4.11. Postcrisis Checklist

counseling point of view. The counselor or Counseling Department must appraise the crisis situation and seek additional support if the need arises. This support can come from community agencies; feeder school districts, if the high school is involved; and other school districts or educational agencies. Another part of the counseling process is its ability to provide parents with information. Many parents want to know the mental and emotional condition of their children. The counselor or Counseling Department must be proactive and prepared to deal with these types of conditions and not react and cause additional concern or trauma in an already difficult situation. See the list provided in Figure 4.10. It is very important to follow these suggestions, especially if you are just beginning to develop a safety and crisis management plan.

What Happens After a Crisis Situation?

The use of a checklist would be a good idea to assist the administrator and the safety and crisis management team after a crisis situation has happened. To be able to refine and identify any unfinished business and to reflect on how well the crisis situation was managed will be a great asset in the revision process and, it is hoped, make the next crisis situation a little less hectic and keep individuals from making any mistakes or perceived mishandling of a difficult situation. Figure 4.11 can assist the building team in identifying follow-up activities that should not be overlooked.

In summary, the principal plays an extremely important part in the safety and crisis management team process. This individual activates the process and directs the actions that need to be taken. Many times, this action will be based on situational decision making. However, proper proactive planning will be a comforting and confidence-building experience. Figure 4.12 identifies and highlights the important procedures that need to be taken during the time of a crisis and needs to be revisited at the conclusion of the situation to ensure that all the necessary steps were taken.

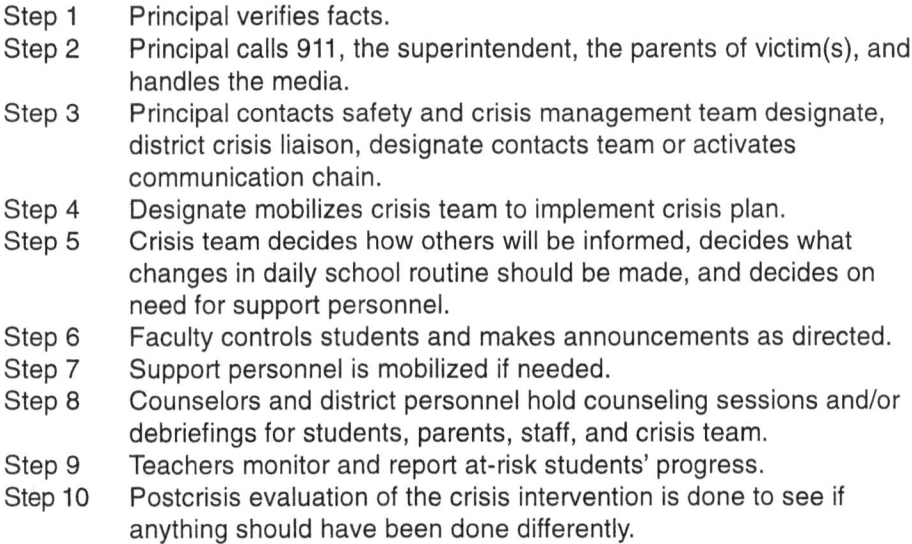

Step 1	Principal verifies facts.
Step 2	Principal calls 911, the superintendent, the parents of victim(s), and handles the media.
Step 3	Principal contacts safety and crisis management team designate, district crisis liaison, designate contacts team or activates communication chain.
Step 4	Designate mobilizes crisis team to implement crisis plan.
Step 5	Crisis team decides how others will be informed, decides what changes in daily school routine should be made, and decides on need for support personnel.
Step 6	Faculty controls students and makes announcements as directed.
Step 7	Support personnel is mobilized if needed.
Step 8	Counselors and district personnel hold counseling sessions and/or debriefings for students, parents, staff, and crisis team.
Step 9	Teachers monitor and report at-risk students' progress.
Step 10	Postcrisis evaluation of the crisis intervention is done to see if anything should have been done differently.

Figure 4.12. Summary of Procedures During a Crisis or Postcrisis

A school/community-based response plan is critical to the efficient handling of a crisis situation. It is imperative that school personnel become familiar with the guidelines and procedures for handling crisis situations. This also includes effective communication both externally and internally.

Step 10: Distribute the Safety and Crisis Management Plan

Once the plan has been developed and approved by the board of education or board of directors, each member of the safety and crisis management team—each administrator, each board member, and each faculty and staff member—should receive a copy. If there are financial resources available, a crisis management flip chart that details the procedures and guidelines for an identified crisis at a quick glance should be developed, printed, and posted in each classroom.

If finances are available, a brochure should be developed that explains the purposes and basic procedures that parents and community members should follow if a crisis situation should happen. Disseminating this basic information will reduce confusion and frustration at the crisis point. This will aid the school, administration, and staff when calmness needs to prevail. Becoming proactive and developing a sound safety and crisis management plan that covers as many potentially dangerous and crisis situations as possible with good, sound management practices will enable parents and community patrons to generate a great deal of confidence and trust in the administration, faculty, and staff when difficult situations arise.

Part Two

Critical Components for Dealing With Crises

Chapter Five

Being Sensitive to Student and Staff Needs

Principal Greg Criswell and his crisis management team have had a difficult past few days as they have had to handle a student death crisis. The student was a popular senior who was class president, girls' basketball team captain, a National Honor Society student, and active in youth community organizations, and she had just received the Governor's Award on Youth Leadership. There was a movement within the community to secure a larger facility to handle the funeral because the local church the family attended was small and unable to handle the expected size of the funeral ceremony. Local community leaders approached Principal Criswell to see if it would be possible to use the gymnasium during the school day for such a ceremony. Mr. Criswell, along with faculty, staff, and students, has been deeply touched by the death of this student, and there are genuine concerns about the emotional state of the individuals affected by this traumatic incident.

How would you handle this situation?

This chapter is crucial to the development of students, whether at the elementary or secondary level.[1] As an administrator and member of the crisis team, understanding and addressing special needs is a monumental project and process in dealing with crisis management situations. Individuals who are coping with grief and are trying to resolve personal loss need additional attention and care. This is the case whether they are staff members or students. The safety and crisis management team that proactively anticipates these situations will have a dramatic impact on the staff and students who are in need of such services.

Addressing the Needs of Staff and Students—Faculty Responsibilities

When a tragedy or crisis occurs, the building administrator has the responsibility of announcing the situation to the student body; or teachers will often be given the responsibility of announcing the situation to each class. They must choose an appropriate way to present the information to the students. It is important to take into consideration the age level and of the students and their closeness to the individual or situation. Sensitivity on the part of the teacher is critical when addressing the situation. Anticipation of an emotional reaction to the information should be foreseen and planned for. It is a good idea to rehearse the giving of this information, if possible. If the person giving this information is emotional or close to the individual or incident, another staff member could be present or even make the announcement.

Altering the Curriculum During Times of Crisis

Faculty who engage students in class activities get children involved in a productive activity and hence direct and contain emotions. This also provides opportunity to rid a child of any potential guilt and reduce the possibility of anger.

It is wise to alter the curriculum or lesson during an emotional time for students to avoid continuing or escalating any stressors or emotional outbreaks. An effective teacher should use the opportunity to help students develop and refine their coping skills. All people, young or old, need to understand their feelings and gain the ability to cope with their emotions.

Certain academic and extracurricular activities give students the opportunity to improve their skills and coping ability. English, art, music, and physical activities are a few such courses and activities. The ability to write and communicate emotions has great emotional release capabilities. Students who draw, paint, or perform other forms of art also have the opportunity to release built-up emotions and frustrations. Music can also establish a reflective mood, helping children to understand life and the living process. Finally, students who engage in physical activity can release their frustrations and stress, enabling them to relax and regroup and to establish coping techniques. Resolving personal conflict and contributing to the mental and physical health of a child during the time of a crisis is an art that many teaching professionals can develop, given a little thought and sensitivity. Remember, returning a child or group of children to a normal setting will aid in the learning process and allow meaningful interactions for both the teacher and student(s) to continue.

Faculty Emotions During a Crisis Situation

Many faculty find it difficult to control their own emotions during times of crisis or grief. It is difficult at times to hold back your emotions and even tears when situations develop and you experience a tightening of the throat or a feeling of anxiety. Students can accept a human emotion from another individual, and it may be the catalyst for them to release the built-up emotions that have been causing them stress or frustration. These times are not embarrassing situations, they are human situations.

Students' Reactions to Crisis Situations

It is certain that reactions to crises and traumatic situations can be expected from students as well as staff members. The impact will be different depending on the grade level and age of the students. Primary-age children are usually the least affected unless the children were very close to the person who died or situation that happened. A more reassuring discussion would need to take place to alleviate the young students' fears and concerns. If the teacher feels uncomfortable about presenting this type of information to very young children, community resource people or other staff members with a more comprehensive background in dealing with these situations should be considered.

Middle school and junior high school students are easily caught up in emotionalizing an event or situation. Students at this age level handle crisis and trauma situations in different ways. Some will become extremely emotional, whereas others will become defiant and still others may appear to be unaffected. Students at this age are already on an emotional roller-coaster, and situations that are emotionally charged may have an exaggerated effect on their ability to cope with and handle a difficult situation. Faculty and staff should expect this as a normal reaction of the grief cycle and be prepared with constructive activities and counseling to deal with the situation. With a sensitive and understanding teacher, the situation of a child overreacting and/or becoming a discipline problem could be minimized or possibly averted.

Many teenagers understand the reality of death. However, many others believe that death or crisis situations happen only to others and never to themselves. When this belief is shattered, there is usually a sobering and reflective period. Individuals work through situations, and many times the crisis becomes a personal growth experience. Faculty and staff who work with teenagers believe it is important to view with the student the issue of death and how individuals have responded to crisis situations. A discussion on how people rebuild their lives after a crisis could be informative and appropriate for this age level. This discussion gives hope that the individual can return to a positive state of equilibrium and regain the spirit of living a happy, successful, and full life.

At whatever grade level a teacher or staff member finds himself or herself, the person in charge needs to be alert to the emotional state of the students. For example, when discussing a recent crisis the teacher should be aware of any excessive silence or withdrawn tendencies of children. Students who undergo severe distress should be escorted to individuals who are trained in crisis therapy or emotional distress. In most cases, the school counselor would have the most knowledge and experience with these types of situations. Additional community resources may need to be secured to assist the school with difficult situations.

Allowing Students to Attend Memorial or Funeral Services

Allowing students to attend and/or participate in memorial or funeral services sends the message that life has meaning and is worth living. Each individual has a value and is loved and remembered in many different ways. The worth of attending such a function may have a very profound educational impact on students as well as adults. There will be little positive education accomplished until students and adults have had an opportunity to process the grief and shock of the crisis and possible loss of life. To hurry the process before an appropriate grieving process and procedure takes place will only create undue pressure on students and resentment of school personnel.

From time to time, school administrative personnel will be asked to hold a memorial or funeral service on school property. Such is the case when there is a popular student or faculty member involved, in cities, and in school buildings that hold significant memories for families of students or faculty members who have died. These situations create concerns for administrators and school personnel. They truly affect the educational process of the entire building and the students of that building. In the event of an elementary-age child's death, the impact may have little effect, and all the students may not need to be involved in the memorial or funeral service. However, as the students mature, they realize that students, faculty, staff, and other adults become involved in the process. As students become older, their social spheres increase and the death of a friend or loved one may affect a larger proportion of the school community.

As a determination of an appropriate site within the school campus is considered, one needs to reflect on more than just the memorial or funeral service itself. Where to hold it is an important decision. Anticipating the size of the service will dictate the need and size of the facility. An outdoor service could be considered, weather permitting and if the size of the facility is appropriate for the service.

An effective way some individuals cope with grief is by active participation in the memorial or funeral service. Students who are a part of

Elementary orientation
  Procession by Safety Patrol Color Guard or other appropriate student group
  Opening remarks by appropriate individual or student
  Invocation if desired
  Reflective message(s)
  Closing remarks
  Recessional

Middle school, junior high, or high school orientation
  Musical prelude
  Opening remarks
  Invocation if desired
  Music by choral group or band
  Message(s) of reflection and/or remembrance (two or three people; can be a mixture of students, faculty, or close friends and loved ones)
  Musical number (solo or group)
  Closing remarks

All grade level orientation
  Opening remarks
  Brief message
  Planting a tree/dedication of a school memorial
  Closing remarks

Figure 5.1. Sample Memorial Service Programs

the service, including the planning of such an event, may benefit. If capable, students who become involved receive a sense of completion and letting go of any further grief. Continuing memories remain but are embraced with positive feeling and fondness for the deceased individual. Should school personnel be asked to speak at memorial or funeral services, trusted counselors or the principal may be appropriate representatives. A clergy member who understands the necessity of a nondenominational service or a person who is an inspirational speaker may be appropriate choices to consider for such an event. Figure 5.1 will provide some suggestions and samples for memorial service programs held on school grounds.

Family members of the deceased student or school personnel should not be involved in the planning of the memorial service. The attendance and participation should be considered but not mandated. If the family wishes to attend the memorial service, obscure seating may be considered so as not to draw attention to family members. This way, if family members become emotional they may be able to leave the service with little notice.

Teachers of students who will be attending the service have an opportunity to prepare the students and try to develop an understanding of what is going to take place. This should be viewed as a teachable moment—an opportunity that, it is hoped, does not come too often. However, when it does, the teacher should not dismiss the opportunity to provide a valuable educational experience for each child.

Do not panic—take a deep breath and carry on.
Appoint a spokesperson.
Develop a written statement concerning the incident or crisis.
Contact the press before they contact you.
Develop media-on-campus guidelines and restrictions.
Do not refuse to speak to the media.
Do not overreact or exaggerate the situation.
Give only factual and verified informational statements.
Do not lie.
Do not try to avoid blame by using a scapegoat.
Stress positive action taken by the school district.
Do not delay sharing what information you have, but make sure you are sharing facts.
Do not bluff, ad-lib, or talk off the record.
Do not deviate from communication policy or agreed-on statements.
Do not argue with media personnel.
Do not project a primary interest in protecting the school's reputation at all costs.
After the incident or crisis has passed, do not avoid the announcement of changes that may have been made.

Figure 5.2. Guidelines for Handling the Media

Half-Mast Flag Guidelines

From time to time, school administrators may be approached about the use of a half-mast flag in memory of a deceased student or staff member. In many situations, the administrator may choose to fly the flag at half-mast. This has a calming and reflective effect on students and other individuals who knew the deceased and wish to memorialize the individual or crisis in this way. The administrator should, however, not allow the flying of the flag at half-mast to be prolonged in a way that it will detract from the remembrance of the individual or individuals.

When Informing the Media

The first rule is, do not panic! The media can work to the school's benefit during a crisis and actually assist in disseminating information about the incident or situation. Figure 5.2 is a detailed guideline to assist you in handling the experience well.

When working with the media, it is imperative to keep a positive attitude, even in the face of disaster. The pressure of the media may become very intense, and your calmness must prevail if you are to get through the crisis without a personal negative effect. Being proactive and anticipating the worst will assist you in making intelligent decisions before the pressure of the crisis and then having to make an important decision on the spur of the moment. Proactive and reflective administrators are less likely to make "fatal errors". Fatal judgmental and decisional errors are caused, in most cases, by reactive administrative decisions pressured by outside environments demanding to know all of the information surrounding the crisis or specific incident. Fatal errors can be

- "On a field trip today involving _____ grade students, the school bus that the students were riding was involved in an accident, _____ miles north of Highway _____. Rescue units are on the scene and are transporting students to nearby hospitals. Three teachers and the assistant principal are also on the scene of the accident at this time. A special hotline has been established for parents to call for more information. The number is _____-_____-_____. Our crisis team has been activated to help students, staff, and families. More information will be released as it is made available."

- "A gang-related fight and shooting took place on the playground of _____ Elementary School last evening. Two high school students were injured with no fatalities. Police and school authorities are investigating at the present time. No other information is available. Since the students involved in this incident attend _____ High School, the building crisis plan has been activated and the following actions have already been initiated:

"Parent hotline has been activated.
The number is ____-____-_____.

"District and community service agencies have been activated to assist individual students and families.

A review of school and district policies relating to gang activity on school grounds is under way."

Figure 5.3. Sample Media Statements Concerning Student or Building-Level Crisis

detrimental to your future professional interests. Proactive and reflective preparation can be a catalyst to your sucessful decisions.

A proactive decision by the administration and/or crisis management team would be to develop a template of statements that could be adapted to situations involving students, staff, and crisis conditions. Far fewer problems develop when a well-thought-out statement is written under normal conditions than when one is needed and written under pressure while in a crisis situation. Figure 5.3 provides samples for your consideration in the event that one is needed before you decide to be proactive.

The importance of these sample statements is that they convey a feeling and belief that the school is on top of the situation and is doing everything possible to alleviate any traumatic and personal grief to individuals who may be involved. The need for comfort and confidence is given to those individuals who may be in need of such help or information.

Note

1. Much of the information in this chapter is from Petersen and Straub (1992).

Chapter Six

Prevention Programs and Strategies

During third-period English class, Mrs. DeVries was having difficulty controlling Brian Clark, and there was an exchange of harsh words. Brian alluded inappropriately to Mrs. DeVries's female characteristics and called her a b____. Mrs. DeVries became irate, and the brief exchange turned into a hostile exchange of words with the student threatening Mrs. DeVries with bodily harm. Mrs. DeVries, becoming nervous and frightened, ordered Brian to the office of Mr. McKenzie, who handled student discipline.

How could Mrs. DeVries have handled this situation more appropriately without direct confrontation?

School districts around the nation have experienced an escalation of crime and violence among students. Personal safety of students and staffs have become high priorities, and many districts have started to involve community agencies and resources in helping to provide solutions to this growing problem. Throughout the first five chapters, you have been told how to develop a crisis plan, how to plan for a crisis when (not if) it happens, who should be on the crisis team, and how to understand and address the special needs that develop during a crisis.

A crisis does not always mean that an unpredicted or accidental situation has happened. Crisis situations can developed from a preplanned, well-thought-out criminal act that has been orchestrated by school or community gangs, the purpose of which can be totally to disrupt the educational process and safe environment of the school.

Preparing the Faculty to Deal With Crime and Violence

The preparation of teachers entering the teaching field leaves a great deal to be desired in dealing with today's societal problems of crime and violence. Teachers, as professionals in the education arena, are not trained to deal with difficult or violent students. It is left up to the individual teacher to fend for himself or herself in confronting and controlling misbehaving or violent students.

Armed with the plans and information that have been discussed in the previous chapters, you will be well on your way to realizing your goals for safe schools through prevention rather than reaction to crime and violence. In developing the district's or building's prevention programs and strategies, remember the premise, "Perception is reality." By sending the strong message that the action plan conveys—*We are serious about having safe schools*—you are assuring your staff and students that the district, from the board of education down to the student, is involved in this proactive approach.

The presence of weapons on campus places the entire academic community at risk and makes everyone a potential victim. An example of this occurred in 1994 when a teacher returned to meet his former employer, a superintendent. With his hand extended in greeting, the superintendent was fatally shot six times. A national survey of a leading life insurance company in 1993 found that 1 in 4 students and 1 in 10 teachers said they had been victims of violence on or near school property. But more important than recognizing the problems that weapons and violence in school cause is the development of effective strategies to deter and prevent such problems. The strategies that are presented in this chapter include training educators in weapon detection, confrontation techniques, and violence diffusion; providing adequate supervision both in and outside of the classroom; and teaching prosocial skills within the curriculum to promote a positive campus climate and to foster interpersonal success in conflict resolution. If we as professionals are going to control the tide of fistfights turning into gunfights, then making campuses safe must become everyone's responsibility: parents, educators, law enforcers, judges, youth-serving professionals, and students.

Although school officials are concerned about all weapons, knives, guns, and explosive devices present the greatest risk to both students and staff. Conservative estimates indicate that as many as 100,000 students carry a gun to school. The Centers for Disease Control and Prevention consider the problem of weapons use among youth to have reached epidemic proportions. An effective weapons/violence reduction strategy must be multidisciplinary, comprehensive, politically sensitive, and practically relevant. Both districtwide consistency and a measure of local autonomy are needed, just as with the development of the safety and crisis management plan.

One of the most effective methods of detecting the presence of weapons and violence on campuses is using tips from students. A toll-free anonymous hotline can encourage this type of communication about reporting criminal activity. One large urban school district increased from 30 tips to 200 tips per day within the first month using the hotline communication network. Another school district solved a series of bomb explosions in restrooms within 25 minutes through the school's Crimestoppers tip/reward program. Yet another district has homeroom teachers emphasize the personal safety aspect of students reporting weapons and crime as a way of doing themselves and the perpetrators a favor. The teacher is the key to developing a climate at school where each student feels responsible to report any criminal or violent behavior. Also, having resource officers who are trained local police or district law enforcement police officers on campus can establish rapport with students and provide an effective communication with students who will then confide in them and report criminal activity.

The Use of Sweeps and Searches

Schools frequently have used a variety of types of sweeps and searches to confiscate weapons. School officials who conduct such searches should receive training regarding reasonable suspicion to understand the parameters of a legal search. The use of searches touches on two very innovative techniques. The school district of San Diego City Schools was the first in the nation to begin eliminating student lockers in 1982. At that time, a "no student locker" statement and policy went into effect. Figure 6.1 elaborates on the San Diego program. If a district finds the San Diego strategy to be unacceptable for its own district, students should be given notice that the lockers belong to the school and that they will be checked regularly for health and safety reasons. Lockers are a privilege, not a right.

Elsewhere, some districts have bought two sets of books, one for home and one for the classroom, this has worked well for schools in which students may not carry book bags. Some schools allow only clear plastic or mesh book bags to be used.

Other types of searches such as K-9 searches have been very successful. District safety and security directors who have conducted this type of search report that the dogs' sense of smell is so keen that they can detect gunpowder, explosives, alcohol, and drugs, including caffeine. The U.S. Supreme Court has ruled that no warrant is needed. The process is as follows: (a) The dog alerts its master; (b) the student is summoned; (c) the officer asks permission to search; and (d) if the student says no, the officer tells the student that the parents will be summoned and the police will impound the property until a judge determines probable cause.

Whether locker, desk, bag, item, or car, many school districts have found this type of search a detraction, and where it has been put into practice it has decreased the size of illegal property seized. The K-9 program has reduced the amount of contraband on campuses, but not on the individual student or person. The courts have ruled that dogs are not

San Diego City Schools
Police Services Department

In 1982, San Diego City Schools was the first school district in the nation to begin the process of eliminating student lockers. During the course of the district's school policy for investigation and responding to several criminal activities in and around the lockers, it was determined that lockers were a major contributor to crime and violence in our schools.

Once a school uses this deterrent strategy, a significant reduction in criminal activity takes place, thus enhancing school safety in the following areas by reducing

1. Tardiness to class
2. Conflicts and fights (as everyone knows, many fights occur in the locker rooms)
3. Vandalism, graffiti, theft, and arson
4. Availability of weapons and contraband
5. Loss of books
6. Sexism (X-rated messages are placed in lockers via graffiti and notes)
7. Racism (hate crime remarks are placed in lockers via graffiti and notes)
8. Monetary losses due to lost or stolen books

The fact that students now carry their belongings in a backpack promotes more interaction/vigilance and better student and campus supervision.

Due to the savings, as a result of the above reductions, some schools have bought two sets of books, one for home and one for the classroom.

A districtwide policy is not in place at this time. The decision is left up to the site principal. However, over 90% of our secondary schools have closed down lockers. They are only allowed in P.E. dressing rooms.

Figure 6.1. Program for No Student Lockers
SOURCE: San Diego City Schools. Used with permission.

allowed to sniff individuals. A model detailing the structure and methodology of a district that used this practice is shown in Figure 6.2.

The Use of Metal Detectors

One of the most popular and controversial methods for reducing crime and violence by confiscating weapons is the use of metal detectors. Using them to screen students at the entrance of schools is time-consuming and labor intensive. Most schools are not designed to make front-entrance screening very realistic, especially on a campus with several buildings. Also, the screening of over 2,000 students requires approximately 2 ½ hours and takes several security personnel. However, metal detectors are

The Board of Trustees (Board) of the _____ School District is committed to providing students and employees with schools and workplaces that are free of drugs and weapons. To that end the Board prohibits the presence of drugs, controlled substances, weapons of any type, explosive devices, and alcohol or any other intoxicant (as those terms are defined by state or federal law or District policy) on District property or at any District-sponsored event. This prohibition applies to employees, students, patrons, visitors, and any other person.

All persons are responsible for the security of any vehicle, locker, desk, bag, or other item they possess or bring onto District property or to a District-sponsored event. No person shall possess, place, keep, or maintain any article or material that is prohibited by law or District policy in items, lockers, vehicles, desks, or bag assigned to them or under their control while on District property or at a District-sponsored event.

In an effort to keep the workplace and schools free of drugs and weapons, the District may use specially trained nonaggressive dogs to sniff out and alert to the presence of those substances prohibited by law or District policy. These inspections shall be unannounced and will be made at the discretion of the program coordinator.

Under no circumstance will a dog be allowed to sniff the person of a student, employee, patron, visitor, or anyone else while on District property or at any District event. This prohibition extends to and includes demonstrations.

The dogs shall not be used in rooms occupied by persons except the handler and District officials or for demonstration purposes.

When used for the purpose of demonstration, the dog may not sniff the person of any individual and must be well separated from the audience.

The dog may be used to sniff the air around lockers, desks, bag items, or vehicles that are on District property or at a District-sponsored event.

Only the dog's official handler will determine what constitutes an alert by the dog. If the dog alerts on a particular item or place, the person having the use of, brings onto District property, or is responsible for that place or item will be called to the scene to witness the search. All searches shall be made in compliance with District policy and applicable law.

In the event the dog alerts on a locked vehicle, the owner or person bringing it onto District property shall be asked to open it for inspection. Refusal to open the item for inspection may result in referring the matter to law enforcement officials, disciplinary action including but not limited to suspension or termination of employment for employees and suspension or expulsion for students, and loss of parking privileges on District property for both student and employee. Visitors or patrons may be banned from District property.

Discovery of a prohibited substance may result in referral to law enforcement for disciplinary action including but not limited to termination of employment for employees and referral to law enforcement or disciplinary action in keeping with District policy for students.

Students shall be informed of this policy at the beginning of each school year. Employees shall be notified of this policy at the beginning of their employment with the District and thereafter at the beginning of each school year.

Figure 6.2. Sample Policy for the Use of Dogs to Search for Contraband on District Property

becoming less expensive: Walk-through magnetometers cost over $2,000 and X-ray machines to screen bags cost over $20,000, whereas hand-held detectors can be purchased for under $200. Metal detectors can be especially effective when security personnel can control the perimeter of an area, such as a gym or stadium, and force everyone to enter through a single entrance. Detectors are also helpful when searching an individual because they are less intrusive than a pat-down search. The former director of security for the Detroit Public Schools presents a balanced view of the use of metal detectors based on widespread use since 1985. The former director states that although everyone thinks of metal detectors as the be-all and end-all, they are just another deterrent. Using metal detectors does alert people to the problem.

When people judge the use of metal detectors as harsh, a former chancellor of New York City Public Schools says having guns and weapons in school is harsh.

To be effective, metal detector use must be part of a larger, more comprehensive prevention policy. The courts have supported metal screening based on an administrative search doctrine. The use of metal detectors sends a strong message to students and the community that the school district recognizes the problem of weapons on campus and is serious about ending it.

Vandalism in the Building or on Campus

Vandalism prevention, including graffiti deterrence techniques is accomplished through swift removal. A photograph should be taken before the graffiti is removed for use as evidence for disciplinary or criminal action when offenders are identified. Also, photographs are invaluable for analyzing the graffiti for possible gang identification. Police should be called in to interview suspects to send a message that graffiti will not be tolerated. Principals with the most success in eliminating gang activity remove the graffiti within a few hours. Some school districts encourage school pride through "Saturday Night Paint Parties" to paint over graffiti. The students who participate in these cleanup activities are among the most valuable resources in fighting vandalism, often using telephone hotlines to report. Principals are changing student attitudes through participation in school pride activities and antivandalism programs. Some district administrators have handed a paintbrush to a first offender and ordered him or her to spend that Saturday night painting over the graffiti.

An anti-vandalism technique that has worked in the San Diego City Schools, despite criticism from the opposite camp that lights deter vandals, was the "darkened school/no lights program" (Figure 6.3). Each school district, administrator, and community needs to come to its own conclusion as to the worth and benefit of such a deterrence program. Administrators who fail to evaluate techniques like the darkened school program risk miscalculating a community's perception about such a change from what seems to be the right thing to do.

School districts that wish to reduce vandalism and theft by implementing the darkened school program should:

San Diego City Schools
Police Services Department

Utility companies throughout the country have done a superb job of brainwashing the general public that lights prevent and deter crime. It is not true. San Diego Schools, upon the recommendation of Alex Rascon, Jr., Director, conducted a pilot study in 1982 on three school levels: elementary, junior high, and senior high. These three schools were in high-crime areas and were constant targets of vandalism and theft. The pilot study required the following:

(a) That the custodian turn off all interior and exterior lights at the completion of their shift each night

(b) That the custodian secure all exterior and interior lights to include fans, blowers, heaters, and air conditioners for weekends and holidays

(c) That entries by staff be minimized on need-be basis for weekends and holidays

To the best of our recollection, the study showed a monthly savings of approximately $380.00 for the elementary school, $800.00 for the junior high school, and $1,900.00 for the senior high school. In addition to the savings of kilowatt hours, we noticed a decrease in break-ins, vandalism, and theft.

As a result of this study, the superintendent ordered all lights to be turned off in all schools and facilities. The concept of "Who is afraid of the dark" works! It defies the concept of policing that everyone is accustomed to, including the police. In our surveys, we find there was sufficient lighting from the street lights for people to walk on the sidewalks surrounding the schools. We did not have to modify any lighting whatsoever to accommodate the communities at large. It took us approximately three years to fully implement the program in getting staff, police, and the community in tune with the concept that if you see a light come on after hours, call school police.

Figure 6.3. Darkened School Program
SOURCE: San Diego City Schools. Used with permission.

1. Promote a school Neighborhood Watch program through flyers.
2. Install a districtwide fire and intrusion alarm system.
3. Solicit total cooperation from school district employees, communities, and the police.

It was reported that San Diego schools saved approximately $1 million a year in utility costs. They found fewer and fewer people on campuses during darkened hours. Consequently, losses due to vandalism and thefts were reduced by better than 30%. The school district police department receives over 1,100 calls a year from community members because of promotional efforts on the school Neighborhood Watch programs.

Developing a Student Assistance Program

Targeting at-risk students who have had a history of community violence or criminal activity and who are potentially violent and then developing a student assistance program will assist in a proactive way to reduce the potential for a crisis. A student assistance team (SAT) is developed to work within the school building or to develop appropriate outside agencies to help develop relationships for prevention, intervention, and recovery of problem students. These programs are effective because there is safety in numbers. A teacher no longer ignores problems because he or she is afraid to report them or does not know for sure what is going on. A team effort is used so that the decision to offer intervention of discipline measures is not just one person's judgment. The assistance team receives a report from a staff member, who contacts the student, coach, counselor, other teachers, bus driver, and so forth. The team then analyzes the record of the student to identify any pattern of activity. A counselor meets with the student to discuss concerns that have been identified. All of the information is then directed to the SAT to determine what the problem is and what would be the appropriate next step(s). Possibilities include calling the parent, referring to an outside agency, or something in between. This program eliminates "enabling" the student to continue with unacceptable behavior by focusing on the exact cause instead of making excuses for the behavior and ignoring the real problem. Hard issues are dealt with in a thorough way. Teachers and school counselors do not have the time to handle such in-depth intervention. This type of early identification can save a student from a lifetime of frustration turned to violence.

In developing a SAT, a number of questions need to be asked. Answering the following seven questions will assist the administrator or school in developing a comprehensive SAT program.

Question 1: What is a student assistance program?

Figure 6.4 gives an overview of a student assistance program and the referral process.

Question 2: What are the basic functions of the student assistance program?

There are six basic functions. First, identify a problem or concern. Second, gather and assess data. Third, determine whether to make a referral or other appropriate intervention. Fourth, maintain the appropriate use of the continuum of care for the student. This function shows the student and family that the school cares about what happens in the future. Fifth, identify and support the maintenance of changes that are sought through the assistance program. Finally, provide a case management situation where the

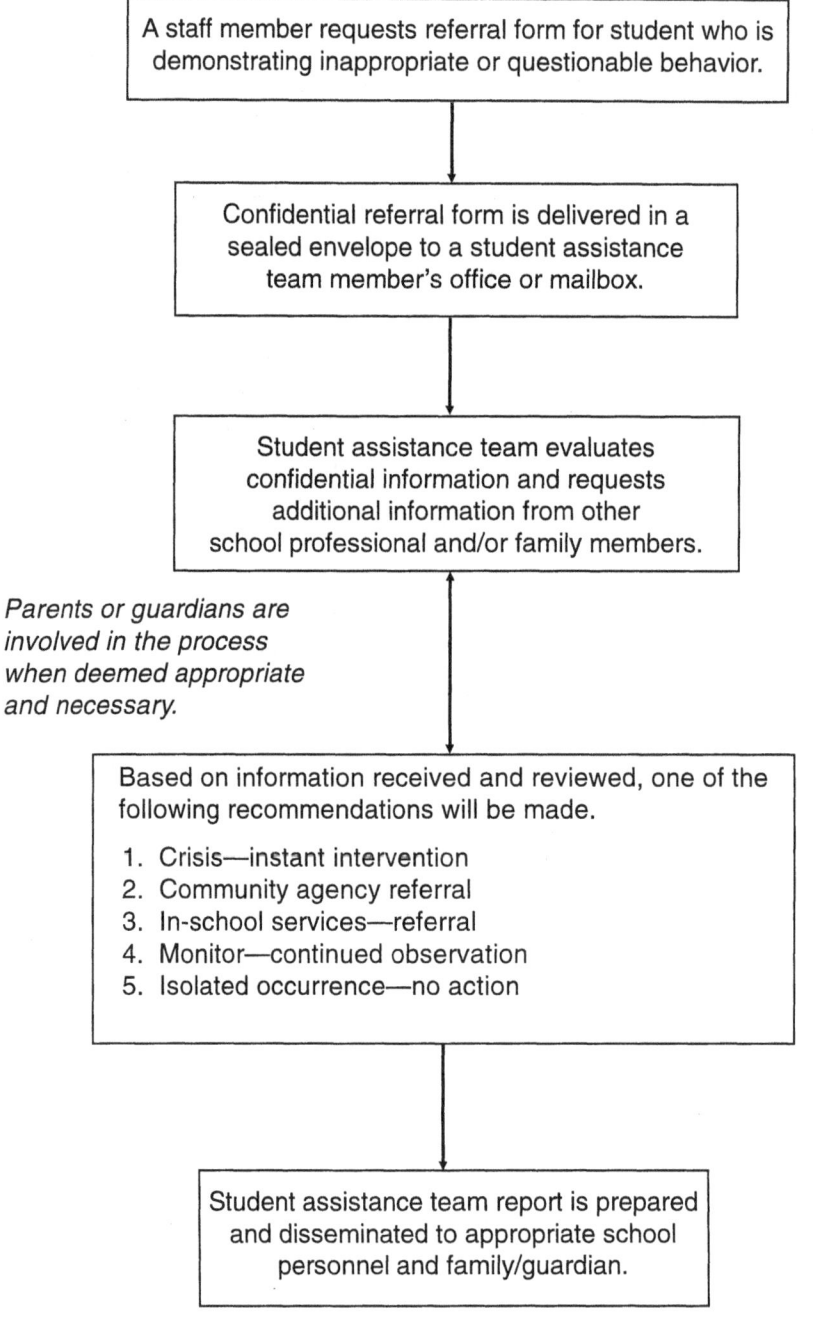

Figure 6.4. Student Assistance Program and Referral Process

child is identified and periodic review can be sought to assist where needed if reoccurrences are identified.

Question 3: What is a student assistance team?

A SAT is made up of energetic individuals who believe they can make a difference in the lives of students with problems. The team provides the leadership in the student assistance program.

Question 4: Who typically serves on the student assistance team?

The building principal and/or assistant principal, guidance counselor, and at least three teachers serve on the team. If a districtwide SAT is desired, a building principal and/or assistant principal, guidance counselor from each building, and at least three teachers per building serve on the team. Also, districts are encouraged to include representatives from the noncertified staff as well.

If large districts develop such a program, there may be a need to develop numerous assistance teams centered around geographic areas or zones within the district. The district can be flexible in its developmental organization of such a team(s).

Question 5: What is the role of the student assistance team districtwide?

In prevention:
- Review and help plan for development of comprehensive prevention programming.

In intervention:
- Review school policies and recommend necessary changes to administration for approval and board adoption.
- Provide or arrange for inservice training for full staff.
- Review and develop/select necessary intervention materials.
- Provide for two-way communication regarding intervention programs.

In recovery:
- Review and help develop quality recovery support programs, groups, and procedures.

Question 6: What is the role of the assistance team in each building?

Overall:

- Help facilitate any of the groups related to the alcohol/drug program (prevention, intervention, and recovery).
- Help maintain awareness of the need for and continued commitment to the range of alcohol/drug programs (prevention, intervention, and recovery).

In prevention:

- Review and help implement quality prevention programs in the school and support quality prevention programs in the community.

In intervention:

- Collect data for assessment phase.
- Attend case reviews on referred students.
- Assist in preparing key staff to participate in actual intervention conference.

In recovery:

- Review and help implement quality recovery support programs, groups, and procedures.
- Educate staff on how to be of assistance to recovering students.

Question 7: What roles do the rest of the staff play in relation to the assistance team?

In prevention, staff members:

- Implement effective prevention curricula or programs, as appropriate.
- Make suggestions to the assistance team on ways to improve the prevention program.
- Update assistance team on progress of prevention program.
- Help support prevention efforts community-wide.

In intervention, staff members:

- Respond to assistance team requests for specific observable data/symptoms.
- Refer students to the SAT.
- Participate in an intervention with a student for whom there is firsthand data and concern.

In recovery, staff members:

- Provide encouragement and support to the recovering student, as appropriate.
- Gently confront student with observed, objective indicators of potential relapse, as appropriate.
- Notify assistance team of observed indicators of potential relapse.
- Support the recovering student by releasing him or her to recovery support group, as appropriate.

In addition to developing a SAT, an administrator who implements this type of program will need to answer a few other types of questions: What are the school's responsibilities in implementing a student assistance program? What are the counselor's responsibilities in implementing a student assistance program? What are the teacher's responsibilities in implementing a student assistance program? Let's answer each of these questions.[1]

What are the school's responsibilities in implementing a student assistance program?

- Observe and document behavior and school performance.
- Establish and train a voluntary assistance team of staff members representative of the school to develop and implement a referral procedure for intervening with at-risk students.
- In compliance with federal confidentiality laws, secure records in a confidential area apart from a student's cumulative file.
- If appropriate, use progressive disciplinary steps to resolve the problem prior to referring the student to the student assistance program.
- Advise the student of the availability of the student assistance program during each disciplinary meeting or other setting.
- Consult and coordinate with the student support team.
- Refer to the student assistance program when a student requests help or a need is indicated.
- Recommend an assessment to the parents if the preassessment dictates it.
- Assist in developing and leading support groups.
- Actively promote the program through newsletters, posters, letters, and other advertisements.
- Cooperate with the assistance team in developing treatment plans with outside agencies.

- Support the student assistance program.
- Coordinate ongoing training and awareness for the entire school staff and community leaders.

What are the counselor's responsibilities in implementing a student assistance program?

- Support and coordinate with the services of the student assistance program.
- Develop rapport with the student needing assistance.
- Develop a counseling relationship.
- Clarify consequences of a student's inappropriate behavior.
- Develop a behavior contract with a student when appropriate.
- Explore with students the connection with the disease of chemical dependency and behavioral indicators.
- Support positive behavior.
- Consult with student/family to determine signs and symptoms of behavior.
- Establish and facilitate/cofacilitate support groups.
- Explore the needs of the students.
- Explore the options of students.
- Offer sites for assessments.
- Network with community to access available resources.
- Know limitations of confidentiality issue.

What are the teacher's responsibilities in implementing a student assistance program?

- Recognize signs and symptoms of students at risk for self-destructive behaviors (chemical dependency, depression/suicide, sexual abuse, occult involvement, etc.).
- Clarify negative behavior.
- Define acceptable behavior.
- Become knowledgeable about student assistance programs and their various components: core teams, peer assistance, cooperative learning, and so on.
- Know policy and procedures.
- Be consistent with follow-through.

Elementary Focus	Secondary Focus
More buy-in for parents/staff	Less buy-in for parents/staff
High parental scrutiny	Greater parent distance
Family focus	Peer focus
Child focus	Adult focus
Protecting parents' privacy	Problems are acknowledged
Problem children are in school	Teens may have dropped out
Developing healthy coping skills	Responding to drug crisis
Hard-to-identify symptoms	Easy to identify sick teen
Easier implementation	Harder implementation
Teacher's role: parent, adviser	Teacher's role: lecturer
Educating the whole child	Specialists
Greater change capability	Lesser change capability
Integrated into curriculum	Operated separately

Figure 6.5. How Program Designs Differ for Elementary and Secondary Levels

- Know effective school and community resources.
- Coordinate with the assistance team.
- Know the referral procedure.
- Know personal limitations and own codependency issues.
- Become aware of ways staff members enable inappropriate behavior with their students.

Figure 6.5 shows how a student assistance program will differ in elementary and secondary schools, and Figure 6.6 gives an example of a SAT referral form.

Many school districts, recognizing the problems their students are facing with alcohol, drugs, and other adolescent issues, have established student assistance programs. Unfortunately, after a great deal of publicity, effort, and expense, many school districts have witnessed the failure of their programs. The difference between successful programs and those that become mere "paper programs" is often related to how well districts address the essential issues confronting such programs.

Figure 6.7 lists 25 common reasons that student assistance programs fail. These were identified from the *Student Assistance Journal*. The list is a good reminder why many prevention programs fail.

It is recommended that every student assistance program undergo a yearly self-examination relating to the 25 common reasons for failure so that the program can be appropriately refined. Areas of deficiency that

Student's name: _____ Grade: _____

Date: _____ Class period: _____

Please mark appropriate items:

A. **Academic performance**   *Explanation*
- ☐ Decline in grade earned
- ☐ Incomplete work
- ☐ Work not handed in
- ☐ Inconsistent work/grades
- ☐ Reduction in quality of work
- ☐ Failing subject _____

B. **Classroom performance**   *Explanation*
- ☐ Disruptive
- ☐ Inattentive
- ☐ Lacks concentration
- ☐ Impaired memory
- ☐ Negativism
- ☐ Not attending class
- ☐ Defiance of authority
- ☐ Cheating
- ☐ Fighting
- ☐ Obscene language, gestures
- ☐ Vandalism
- ☐ Tardiness
- ☐ Other (identify)_____

C. **Other behaviors**   *Explanation*
- ☐ Erratic behavior
- ☐ Mood swings
- ☐ Unexplained popularity
- ☐ Disorientation
- ☐ Sudden weight loss or weight gain
- ☐ Defensiveness
- ☐ Daydreaming
- ☐ Talks freely about drug use
- ☐ Associates with known drug users
- ☐ Slurred speech/dry mouth
- ☐ Poor hygiene
- ☐ Glassy or bloodshot eyes
- ☐ Dark glasses
- ☐ Loss of motivation
- ☐ Withdrawal
- ☐ Talking or writing about suicide

V. **Home Environment**   *Explanation*
- ☐ Known or suspected death: _____
- ☐ Known or suspected divorce: _____
- ☐ Known or suspected separation: _____
- ☐ Other:

_____
_____

Figure 6.6. Student Assistance Team Referral Form
SOURCE: Georgia Department of Human Resources and Georgia Department of Education.

Please respond to the following questions:

Have you had a discussion with this student? _____ Yes _____ No

Have parents/guardian been contacted by you? _____ Yes _____ No

Would you like to discuss this situation with a
student assistance team _____ member or _____ team? _____ Yes _____ No

_____
signature of referral person required

For SAT Team Use

Date Received: _____

Date returned: _____

Student's counselor: _____

Figure 6.6. Student Assistance Team Referral Form *(continued)*

are uncovered during a self-examination should be addressed to enhance the overall effectiveness of the program.

Linking to Law Enforcement Agencies

As school districts develop and implement different strategies to curb violence and violent acts by students and staff, many districts have linked themselves with law enforcement agencies. There are basically two alternatives for schools to consider. One is the school resource officer program. This program places a law enforcement officer on your campus who performs all security duties and counsels and educates students and parents. Hired officers are still employed by the city or county municipality, but they serve either full-time or part-time on school campuses. Most of the time, the expenses are shared by the district and municipality, as is the liability relating to each officer.

As in all programs of this nature, there are advantages and disadvantages. One of the advantages is the flexibility of the school district and the municipality to negotiate an agreement on a yearly basis. Usual terms negotiated include costs to be shared, terms of liability to be shared, and how officers will be selected. Some districts and municipalities appoint a committee to review officers recommended by the police department.

Lack of community support

Lack of administrative support

Lack of cooperation with guidance counselors

Lack of cooperation with law enforcement officials

Lack of cooperation with teachers' unions

Lack of cooperation with extracurricular programs

Lack of cooperation with community resources

Lack of communication with other staff

Centralization around a charismatic leader

Sabotage by critics of the student assistance program

Lack of policy about alcohol and other drug use

Lack of adequate coordination

Lack of perceived need for prevention efforts

Lack of honest publicity

Lack of adequate resources

A treatment mentality

Too broad a focus

A "witch hunt" mentality

Lack of confidentiality

Obsessive confidentiality

Isolation of the student assistance program from comprehensive schooling

Lack of honest, open, personal programs

Codependency among student assistance program staff

Lack of support systems for the caregivers

Lack of ongoing revitalization efforts

Figure 6.7. Reasons Why Student Assistance Programs Fail
SOURCE: Reprinted from *Student Assistance Journal* (Sept./Oct. 1988), with permission from Performance Resource Press, Inc., 1270 Rankin Drive, Suite F, Troy, MI 48083; 810-588-773.

Other advantages are that security personnel are trained when they are hired and support officers are usually available when contacted by the district resource officers. Also, there is little ambiguity about the reporting authority; everyone knows the role of the resource officer on campus. There is immediate radio contact to the local police department if the need arises. The most enticing benefit is that although school districts are not in the business of law enforcement, a district has the ability to maintain reasonable order and safety for students and staff.

As with programs of this nature, there are disadvantages and this program is no different. The officers usually report to the chief of police and not to the school board. This may create a dichotomy between the police department's and the school district's mission and goals. There is the possibility that police officers who are assigned to the district will be dismissed or reassigned by the county or municipality, hence leaving the campus without an officer for a period of time or resulting in a less effective officer being assigned to the campus position. If your district overlaps more than one municipality, inconsistent guidelines may develop from school to school. Finally, officers sometimes lack flexibility in dealing with delinquent acts; therefore, make sure that the school district has some input into the hiring of campus security.

A second program involves the school district developing its own police department. This program is used in school districts where crime and violence are high or where liaisons with local police do not work well enough to provide a satisfactory, safe environment. The state of Texas has over 40 such districts with police departments. Advantages to this type of in-house security program lie in the fact that the school police department reports directly to the superintendent of the school district not to the chief of police of the local municipality. Also, the school district defines the role of the officers, and the officers have jurisdiction on all campuses. This is a big advantage where districts are serviced by more than one municipality. Other advantages are that the school district can decide proper dress codes and policy issues—such as the carrying and use of weapons. Officers can be assured that they will be working on a daily basis thus establishing a rapport with students and staff. Officers will be specifically trained to deal with youth problems and situations, and this will provide consistency from school to school in how a class C misdemeanor will be handled. An important advantage of this type of security force is that daily reports of criminal activity can be achieved, and appropriate administrative personnel will be able to provide accurate reports to parents and other school personnel to minimize and control escalating rumors. The reporting mechanism will also provide a way to analyze recurring problems.

On the negative side, it can be costly for a district to have its own security force. There should be a comprehensive planning process, probably done a year in advance, before any implementation is attempted. In this planning process, a sufficient amount of time must be taken to assure that financing such an operation is feasible. Within this budgeting/ planning process, the district should realize the amount of training and the amount of money it will take to equip officers so they will be able to effectively perform their role as security officers. A perceived disadvantage to developing your own security force is that the district administrators may depend on the school district police department too heavily; remember that these people are not miracle workers but individuals who are trained to reduce and, it is hoped, eliminate criminal or violent acts by students and adults while on the school campus. A major disadvantage is that the school district assumes the total liability of the actions of its employees, including the district's police officers.

It is obvious that there are crossover advantages and disadvantages for both school resource officers/liaison officers and school district police department programs. One other consideration, besides lower cost, for choosing the resource officer program is the capability to set up written contracts that can have negotiated terms to meet your needs so you can overcome many of the disadvantages. However, if the funds are available, a school district police department provides the most consistency, flexibility, and control.

If your district does not have a resource/liaison officer or its own police department, it is important that your staff is well trained in security measures so that your building(s) will be reasonably safe and secure. Some areas of concern in schools are the following: breaking up fights, dealing with a violent student(s), handling a student exhibiting violent behavior, and dealing with an angry student.

There is a yearly conference held by the National Association of School Resource Officers that provides training for both officers and school administrators. This training prepares individuals to respond to school violence and crises to maximize the use of law enforcement resources.

Breaking Up Fights

Effective intervention in fights and assaults on school campuses is the responsibility of every employee hired by the district. Peter Blauvelt, in *Effective Strategies for School Security* (1981), says that more teachers and administrators are injured while breaking up fights and assaults than during any other activity. This occurs because the person breaking up the altercation makes several critical mistakes.

"First, the adult runs up to the fight and immediately jumps in the middle of the fracas and starts pulling the combatants apart," Blauvelt points out. "This action offers the kids a free shot at the adult. After all, in the heat of the fight, how could they possibly know that it was a teacher pulling them apart? They thought it was some other student!" (p. 37).

The second critical mistake adults make is that they do not take the time to analyze the fight, Blauvelt notes.

> By jumping right into the middle of the dispute, the adult does not know if one or both of the fighters has a weapon; if the altercation is a staged event—staged for the benefit of the teacher or administrator; if the fight is in the winding-down stage, meaning both kids are pooped; or who the aggressor is. You want to know

Prevention Programs and Strategies 77

who has or is getting the better blows in because that is the person you must watch. (p. 37)

There is no magic formula for breaking up fights, but there are a few suggestions that may help teachers, staff, and administrators to deal with a fight situation.

- Promptly walk, do not run, to the fight so you can visually analyze the situation and mentally form a strategy as you approach the fight.
- The moment you come in sight of the altercation, use your best cafeteria voice and let the world know you are coming and you want this nonsense to stop.
- If possible, while walking to the fight, stop at various classrooms and obtain help from other teachers; make sure someone is sent to the office for additional help.
- Call out to any of the students you recognize and start giving orders: "Mary, go to Mr. Frank's room; Sam, you go to the office and get Mr. Jones; Calvin, go to your locker and get me your science book." It does not matter what you tell the kids to do. Just remember, kids are accustomed to responding to directions, so give them directions.
- Use spectators to divert energy—get them to chant "Stop fighting, stop fighting," or sing some happy song such as "Ring Around the Rosy" to create a situation in which fighting is incongruous.
- If you know the fighters by name, call out each of their names and let them know you know who they are. This may be the time for a little humor. If you can get some of the kids laughing, it will ease the tension.
- Divert attention by shouting, "Hey, who lost this dollar?"
- If you are confronted with a real donnybrook of a fight, get additional help. Do not try to be a hero unless you are prepared.

If you are going to separate two fighters, first be sure that you can do it; that is, be sure you are bigger than they are and have a clear procedure in mind when you start.

- If the fighters are larger than you, or if they are out of control, you may fail in separating the two fighters and you may even get hurt.
- Never restrain one student without restraining the other. Restraining one fighter may open him or her to the attack of the other, which will not win you any points as a peacemaker.
- If you must, let the fight run its course.

- In a real emergency, grabbing the students by their hair will usually stop a fight right away. But taking violent action against a student opens you to counterviolence.

It is often helpful for teachers to help the participants dissipate their emotions by separating them for a period of time. Some procedures for doing so are

- Cool-off corners where fighters are sent not to be punished but to calm down. When they have cooled off, they can leave their corners.
- Deep breathing to relax them (counterconditioning). Have students take slow, deep breaths while you count to 10 and then back to 1 again.
- Hose them down if they are overheated.
- Give them the opportunity to get rid of their anger. Walk them around and give them exhausting physical activities to do.
- Practice cool-down procedures in a class.

Student Anger and Violence

Dealing with the violent student is the speciality of Peter Commanday, coordinator of professional training in New York City's Office of School Safety. He offers workshops on this topic for teachers, security guards, and others. Commanday claims to have personally disarmed more than 400 students during 25 years as a teacher and dean in South Bronx schools—which are among the nation's toughest—while seldom having to resort to physical means.

His advice is to stay cool under verbal abuse and let the student do the talking. The ability to listen to a student's complaints is paramount. Commanday's tactics for dealing with aggressive students are well thought-out. Some of his suggestions include[2]

- Never approach a disruptive student directly because this might trigger a confrontation. Approach on a diagonal course.
- Never point at the student. Look at the bridge of a violent student's nose.
- Do not "jail" a child with his back to the wall. That's done when you talk to someone of lesser rank. Put your back against the wall, too. Then you can talk equal to equal, friend to friend.
- Remember that no one can go from the boiling point to cool instantly. Aim to change the tone of the crisis gradually.
- Never say, "Calm down," "Relax," or "What's your problem?" What you are saying is that what's upsetting the person is not important to you. Instead, say things like "What's up?" "Tell me everything," "I'm going to listen."

- Use a tone of voice that is not accusatory.
- Watch body language. A subtle roll of the shoulders signals that the student is about to swing, so step aside.
- A desk placed in a room at an angle will disorient potential aggressors and be harder for them to leap over.
- Menacing men and boys can always be disconcerted by telling them their flies are open.

Blauvelt and Commanday have given many good suggestions on how to break up fights. Staff members also need to be able to deal with students who exhibit violent behavior. Some suggestions in this area may help.

- Train teachers to identify factors predictive of violent behavior.
  - Evidence of past or continuing violent behavior
  - Evidence of the child being a victim of abuse
  - Evidence of family climate of violence (e.g., verbal threats)
  - Evidence of student being cruel to animals
  - Presence of subculture supporting aggressive behavior
  - Recent release from incarceration
- Train teachers to lessen possibility of violence through arrangement of learning environment.
  - Examine classroom and school for potentially dangerous sites.
  - Plan lessons with little down time.
  - Explain class rules and expectations clearly.
  - Explain consequences of violent behavior.
  - Train teachers not to use punitive or deprecatory methods of speech.
  - Train teachers to use mediation skills in stressful situations.
  - Train teachers not to use any instructions that result in sudden, surprising, or spontaneous events that the student can perceive as dangerous.
- Train teachers to develop classroom procedures to deal with violent behavior if it does occur.
  - Procedures must be in accord with school discipline policies.
  - Procedures should be given to the entire class the first week of school.
- Follow classroom procedures if a student becomes violent or carries a weapon.
  - Tell students to respond to the word *drill* by walking behind teacher or appointee out of the room.

- Tell students not to walk behind or near a violent student(s).
- Assign one student the responsibility of contacting the school office.
■ Teacher responsibilities should include the following:
  - Look for signs of physical evidence of drugs because this may prohibit normal reasoning with a student(s).
  - Determine if classroom should be evacuated right away or at first opportunity.
  - Focus the attention of a violent person on teacher—this can be done by teacher taking two steps back and standing behind desk or furniture.
  - Place hands on desk with thumbs under edge—this will enable teacher to overturn furniture or use for protection if needed.
  - Encourage person with weapon or using violent behavior to leave the room with statements like, "You might want to leave the room now."
  - Always face the person and never block the door.
  - Use gentle tone of voice and ask that weapon be put down.
  - Ask if the person is angry at you.
  - Do not use imperative statements or authoritative voice.
  - Keep eye contact.
  - Give choices, not orders.
  - Keep body language nonthreatening—hands down or on desk but never behind hips or back. Avoid pointing fingers.

Some suggestions for dealing with angry students are designed to help students avoid unnecessary frustrating situations. Some suggestions for on-the-spot actions you can take when you see your student is having a problem are listed below.

Do not angry back. When a student gets angry at you, the first tip is for you to control your own feelings. It will help if you think of your responsibility to teach. Your student probably does not understand the strong feelings building up inside, obviously does not know what to do with them, and may well be frightened by the possibility of losing emotional control. A child will act angrily when the real problem is deeper and more frightening: a feeling of failure, low self-worth, loneliness, boredom, fear, confusion, and even sadness.

Treat the student with respect and give your students the "right" to feel angry. Remember that anger is a natural human feeling. Your student has a right to feel and express anger as well as happiness, joy, sadness, grief, and pain. Remember that anger is different from aggression. Aggression is an attempt to hurt someone or destroy something. It infringes on the rights of others.

Recognize that the temptation to use aggression is a sign that you are feeling weak and helpless toward your student. You are at your wit's end and do not know what to do. Back off, cool down, and try something else. Violence only hurts. Often, it will escalate the situation and influence the student to be even more destructive in his or her behavior.

Catch your student being good. Remember why your student behaves—to feel good. Students of all ages have good feelings when teachers recognize and reward their good behavior.

Ignore inappropriate behavior that can be tolerated. Remember why a student misbehaves—to react to past or present hurts. A student with an emotional wound, like a person with a physical wound, becomes "swollen and inflamed" with fear, hurt, and anger.

Make it easy for your student(s) to be good. Give your student(s) plenty of opportunity for physical exercise to let off extra energy.

Use affection. Sometimes a sudden show of affection will help an angry student regain control.

Say no. To stay within the limits, a student needs a clear idea of what those limits are and needs to be free to operate within them. Set clear limits that you are prepared to enforce. Also, feel free to change them when you think your students are ready for greater responsibility for their behavior.

Explain situations. Understanding a situation can help a student understand the cause of his or her anger and begin to calm down. Your explanation can include telling the child how you feel and asking for consideration.

Help your student(s) realize that angry feelings do not make a person "bad," and in general help your student(s) build a good self-image. If a child is convinced he or she is a "bad" student, then you can be sure the child will act like one. Students need to know they are valued, that they have strengths as well as weaknesses, that they are able to reach their goals, that their angry feelings do not make them bad people.

Teach your student(s) to express anger in words. Talking is an acceptable pressure valve and helps the student avoid "blowing up." Teach your students to put angry feelings into words instead of fists.

Be a good model. Model expressing anger constructively.

Use punishment cautiously. Your rule might be, "Is this punishment educational or just a way for me to let off steam?" Let off steam some other way. Then decide what action is needed to correct your student's behavior.

Use physical restraint carefully. Sometimes, physical restraint is necessary to stop a student from hurting himself or herself or a classmate. Physical restraint is not to be used as a means of punishment or angry behavior or a as chance for other students to ridicule the angry student. Physical restraint is simply a way of saying, "You cannot do that."

When you cannot handle a situation, seek help. Do not hesitate to seek help from colleagues and administrators when you need to.

Talk to yourself. Prepare yourself for the experience by saying such things to yourself as, "I'm good at managing students' anger." Ignore the anger by saying such things to yourself as, "His or her anger is a minor annoyance, not a major catastrophe." Cope with your arousal and agitation by saying such things to yourself as, "Breathe deep, relax, slow your pulse down." Reward yourself for coping successfully by saying such things to yourself as, "You were terrific, you were calm during the whole conversation."

Prevention Strategies

Schools can take other preventive measures that directly involve students in reducing property crime and other threats to school security. For instance, written policies should stipulate that vandalism is a crime, not a prank, and requires a law enforcement response. Policy statements also should specify that bomb threats or bomb placement on school property is viewed as an act of terrorism and indicate community police will respond to these cases.

Repair and replacement funds, established by the school, district, community, or local businesses, are used to pay for repairs after vandalism incidents. Students and community members should know that money unspent at the end of the school year will revert to the school for its chosen use.

Another prevention strategy is to develop student school beautification and improvement projects. It is hoped that these will increase student pride and responsibility. School and community pride programs enlist students, teachers, and community members to achieve excellence, which includes a crime-free environment. Photo, essay, and poster contests can stimulate interest.

Such programs as Adopt-a-School encourage community organizations and businesses to affiliate with a campus to improve its educational or physical image. The community sponsor can contribute leadership and financial support. Also, Youth Crime Watch programs recruit students to report incidents on school campuses and help reduce robberies, thefts, and trespassing. Task forces that include educators, students, community members, and law enforcers, can work to develop community awareness and specific solutions to campus problems. Vandalism forums, sponsored by school and law enforcement agencies and held in the community, inform citizens of the causes and costs of school vandalism. Informational assemblies and curriculum units advise students on the direct costs of vandalism and other school property crimes.

Many schools and districts have extended the use of school facilities to deter vandals. Prospective vandals begin to feel the school is constantly occupied. Community groups, local colleges and universities, and law enforcement agencies can be encouraged to use school facilities on evenings and weekends. If a school or district uses this strategy, school personnel should secure an inventory of equipment and monitor the inventory on a regular basis as well as monitor chemical storage areas.

School and District Response Strategies

When laws and school regulations are violated, schools must employ response measures that will complement law enforcement's efforts:

- Use punishment, counseling, and diversion efforts with students who have a history of school crime.
- Enlist the support of local businesses to help donate cleanup materials when vandalism hits your school.
- Initiate School Watch programs and provide students and community members with telephone numbers to be called if they witness suspicious or criminal behavior. Permit callers to remain anonymous.
- Establish secret witness and reward programs that allow students and community members regular access for reporting incidents while remaining anonymous.
- Negotiate with the city or county to locate and remove school and community graffiti and support intervention and diversion programs for minor offenders and high-risk youth.
- Provide Saturday cleanup and fix-it options for first-time, minor offenders as restitution.
- Recruit students to serve on "rub-out" squads to clean up school or community graffiti immediately after it is discovered.
- Publicize the penalties of suspension or expulsion and arrest for vandalism and graffiti offenses.
- Encourage and assist with the prosecution of those suspected of arson, vandalism, bomb threats, burglary, and theft.

- Repair damage immediately to deny vandals the opportunity to admire their work and to minimize its social impact.
- Establish restitution procedures to identify those guilty of property crimes and to require payment from them for damage caused.

This chapter has attempted to identify concerns and practical problems that cause stress and tension for students, staff, and community patrons. Prevention programs are an important way to educate students and community members about what is happening to their public, tax-dollar-supported educational institutions. Also, school campuses and school districts should look for violence prevention curriculums for adolescents. One such curriculum, developed by Deborah Prothrow-Stith (1991), deals almost exclusively with violence between peers.

Strategies developed in a proactive format allows school administrators and boards of education to develop reasonable solutions and remedies to growing and potentially "fatal" problems for schools. When policies have yet to be developed in this area, administrators and boards of education necessarily find themselves moved into a reactive format, and the possibility of an emotional response, which may incite more incidents, could take place. The moral of this story is plan ahead and be prepared for the unexpected. The unexpected will happen; it is just a matter of when.

Notes

1. The lists of responsibilities are from the Georgia Department of Human Resources and Georgia Department of Education.

2. The suggestions from Commanday were provided by New York City's Office of School Safety.

Chapter Seven

Including Parents as Partners in Prevention

> At 4:27 p.m. on a Thursday afternoon, Mr. Dana Deines, principal of George Washington Carver High School, received a call from a parent notifying him that her son and another boy had not come home after school. Both boys had attended school that day and had been instructed to come home after school. The parents of both boys were very concerned and wanted to know what to do. Mr. Deines called his superintendent and a search was initiated. At 6:37 p.m., the boys were found dead two blocks away from the school. The boys had overdosed on cocaine.
>
> *As principal, how would you handle this situation? How would you use the community resources to assist in this situation and possible future incidents?*

As educators and citizens, we have concerns about the increasing aggressive and violent behavior that we hear about and see within our communities and even within many of our schools. The problem of youth violence is not merely a problem of the schools; it is a community problem that affects the entire fabric of a community's quality of life.

A Community Concern

Many social and civic agencies, organizations, and institutions as well as schools, churches, and politicians are working diligently to address the problem of "kids killing kids." There are certainly many factors that contribute to the increase in youth violence. Our collective challenge and responsibility must be to make every effort to see that our schools are safe places for our students to learn and for our teachers to teach. Although we cannot deny that the problem exists, it is essential that we do not consider the problem to be irreversible or hopeless. It has taken nearly a generation for this social problem to evolve to its present status; however, it need not and must not take another generation to reverse it. Perhaps we should remember the words of Emerson, who said, "This time, like all times, is the best of times, if we but know what to do with it."

First Step for Parents

A first step for parents is to take the Gang Banger Test for Parents, a very simple test that helps parents face reality about their child. Many parents remain in denial and choose not to confront situations, hoping they will go away. As we all know, this will never happen, and in reality the situation usually becomes worse. Figure 7.1 is the short test to help parents identify to what degree their child is involved with gangs.

Three Types of Parents

As we review parents as possible partners in the prevention of crime and violence, we discover that there are three types of parents. Willing and able parents can and would assist the school or district, but are lacking information about what is happening. There are parents who are willing but unable, who have a desire to help where needed but they need direction and training. The final group are those parents who are unable or unwilling to get involved. These parents should not be overlooked but need to be challenged with some individual attention. These parents are discouraged. They do try to help their children but usually have no success. These parents need the support of the school and others as well as the school needing them for support and assistance.

When parents become involved, they can become extremely helpful in prevention programs. Some ways parents can help include the following:

- Help contact other parents of gang-prone youth.
- Telephone habitual truants.
- Work with underachievers or defeated learners as tutors.
- Assist and monitor at-risk students' progress.
- Share information about the history of the community.
- Help in the library, in the supervision of the campus.
- Tape-record materials for students with reading problems.
- Help in vocational classrooms.
- Help with after-school activities like clubs and athletics.
- Identify students with special talents in fine arts, that is, dancing, music, drawing, and refer them to the right sources.
- Arrange meaningful field trips.
- Sponsor school clubs and interest groups.

Parental use only: Not my child?

Circle the best answer

Dress
- A. My child constantly wears all black, blue, or red (sportswear: caps and jackets).
- B. My child constantly wears a mixture of reds with black and blues with black.
- C. My child wears his clothes too large (sagging).
- D. My child doesn't fit any of these categories.

Body (physical appearance)
- A. My child constantly wears his hair in braids or ponytails.
- B. My child has tattoos of the street he lives on, on his body (also teardrop tattoos).
- C. My child has unexplainable scars and bruises on his body.
- D. My child keeps his hair clean-cut, has no scars or tattoos.

Language (oral or written)
- A. My child constantly talks in slang terms (*cuzz, blood, homie, O.G.,* etc.)
- B. My child writes his letters backwards and crosses out or refuses to write certain letters (usually B or C).
- C. My child constantly uses profanity or writes graffiti.
- D. My child speaks and writes normally.

Associates
- A. My child's friends are always older than he is.
- B. My child never lets me meet his friends.
- C. My child seems to care more about his friends than his family.
- D. I know all my child's friends and their activities.

Behavior
- A. My child is constantly in trouble with the law.
- B. My child stays out late and refuses to tell me where he has been.
- C. My child uses disrespectful language in front of me and my friends.
- D. My child is respectful and rarely gets in trouble.

Explanation of lettering system

A = 10 points	42 to 50 = Hard-core gang banger
B = 8 points	31 to 41 = Gang affiliations
C = 7 points	15 to 30 = Wanna-be
D = 1 point	14 or less = Safe zone

- A. Your child has a 99% chance of being a hard-core gang member. Open your eyes and get some help!
- B. Your child is likely to have some gang affiliations but you haven't lost him yet. You may need to take some drastic steps to get your child back. Move out of the neighborhood. Have your child live with a relative. Pray.
- C. Your child is in the wanna-be stage. This is a critical time for you and your child. Pay more attention to the child and immediately correct inappropriate behavior.
- D. Your child is probably not a gang member, but don't take anything for granted. Stay aware of your child's behavior and activities.

Figure 7.1. Gang Banger Test for Parents

SOURCE: Michael Dennis Michael, *Gang Violence: An Eternity of Silence*. Free Minds, Free Spirits, 12721 South Willowbrook Avenue, Compton, CA 90221.

NOTE: The original wording of the test is retained; however, "his or her" can be substituted throughout to indicate that the test can apply to both boys and girls.

- Assist with staff or student publications, that is, newspaper and yearbook.
- Produce a parent-teacher newsletter to inform parents about the school and school activities.
- Assist special education teachers with students with special needs.
- Help students who are taking tests.
- Assist non-English-speaking students to expand their communication skills.
- Share information about other countries and cultures.
- Raise funds for school projects.
- Recruit other volunteers.
- Serve on educational advisory committee.
- Organize environmental improvement projects.

There are many opportunities for parents and others in the community to become involved in the school. It is up to the school to make its needs public. The community may not be aware of the changing school environment and culture or may perceive that the school does not have a need for volunteers. If the community will not come to the school, then the school must go to the community.

Concerns of Parents

One of the many concerns parents have is, "How do I prevent my child from joining a gang?" Involving parents in gang prevention can take on various forms. The involvement may be of primary importance such as extensive home visits or a support service to prevention programs. Whatever the role, working with parents can be justified for many reasons.

- Parents of troubled students can often be at a loss as to how best to help. These parents can be especially receptive to a program that offers support and help. Not all school problems are precipitated by the school environment. It is noted, however, that school can become the natural arena where students can act out feelings against their parents. School problems aggravated by family problems might be best helped by a parent involvement approach.
- Parent involvement approaches recognize the importance of the family in the student's education. The family is the first and one of the primary educators. A parent involvement approach can teach parents to be better educators as well as how to use resources to reinforce gang prevention efforts at home.
- Working with parents can positively affect student behaviors and attitudes. Research has shown that working with parents, especially when combined with student counseling, is an effective way for bringing about behavioral changes in students.

- Studies indicate that working with parents on an ongoing basis can have beneficial effects on the student's achievement level.

Strategies to Help Parents Become Involved

All parents want their children to succeed, but some lack the information or skills as to how to assist and divert them when problems arise. Part of the partners in prevention program is the education of the parents. Some alternative strategies that can be used follow.

- Teach parents to be responsible models.
- Help them establish honest communications—understand your child's feelings.
- Teach them how to set clear standards and stick to them.
- Encourage them to get involved if they see their children begin to have problems.
- Encourage them to know their children's friends—ask to meet them and their parents.
- Encourage them to get involved with the school.
- Encourage them to pay attention to school grades.
- Tell them what the school policy is on gangs, drugs, and so on.
- Provide opportunities for them to get involved with the local police:
  - Report unusual grouping(s) in your neighborhood.
  - Talk to other parents.
  - Establish block parent and crime prevention programs, that is, Neighborhood Watch.

By assisting parents to take a more active role in their children's education and activities, schools will be enabling parents to deal with difficult situations in a positive and cooperative manner. This enables parents to take charge and be responsible parents and citizens. Students want their parents to become involved in their activities, but it is not "cool" to ask. As parents, we become lax in our responsibility for many reasons, some of which are unavoidable, but we must be given the opportunity to become involved when the need arises. The role of the school is to make a serious effort to work with parents as partners and not to perceive parents as problems.

Schools Building Bridges With Parents

An area in which schools and school districts need to do a better job is building bridges to the parents of gang-prone youth. School personnel need to know the families of gang-prone youth and develop good, sound, trusting communication with them. Most parents are very concerned about their children, but many do not know how to cope or how to react properly to adolescent behavior. When they do react, many times it is in a negative way, which fuels negative reactions from their children and drives a wedge farther into the relationship. Another way of building bridges with parents and families is to recruit them as volunteers either during the school day if they are available or for other school events when they are available. Cultural events, for example, are good activities for parents to show their children that they have interests in other things besides confrontation, work, and doing nothing. The school or district may want to start a parenting class to assist parents with coping and communication skills. Many parents are unaware of acceptable communication methods and rely on their emotions to carry them through difficult situations. In most cases, emotions are the last thing you want to show to individuals who already believe that they are doing the right thing. Support groups are another way that concerned parents may develop some understanding and skills to communicate with and try to positively influence their children.

In building these bridges, there may be a need to develop community awareness projects, on gangs or drugs, for example, to alert the community and parents of an existing threat to the school, the community, and their children. Schools that remain in denial as to the condition of the building or district are not doing the community and families of their students any service. You, as an administrator, could be seen as being a real educational leader for the good of students by alerting the community to the gang or drug-related problems that the building or district is facing. While in the reactive mode, there is always a tendency to point fingers as to why the situation got out of hand. Many critics will be looking for scapegoats to justify their position. As a school administrator, you need to be proactive and confront the situation and seek assistance in solving problems. This particular problem you are not going to solve by yourself, so why not be proactive and muster support for the right way to change students' conduct and lives? You just might save a child's life!

As we build these bridges, we need to empower parents to participate with the school in trying to direct the lives of young troubled people. Schools need to take the "we" attitude instead of the "you" attitude. We need to acknowledge frustration with the situations that exist and not try to be all-knowing when it comes to communicating with parents. It is wise to acknowledge and value the parents' input in these matters. Recognizing that the school and parents are working together for the betterment of the school and child will have a lasting effect on the community and its perception of what the school is trying to achieve in the lives of its children.

Another bridge that could be built is that of developing or establishing a Gang Advisory Council for the purposes of seeking input into existing conditions and current situations. With the involvement of family members and others in the community, the school will provide a realistic opportunity to become involved in a serious community concern. A school district also conveys respect when reaching out to parents and the community. Whenever the school has regular communication with parents and the community constituency, it provides a great service and enhances the perception that the school cares.

As you provide these opportunities, the school becomes the "center" of the community and the beacon of light and hope for the future. We need not make any false promises but be able to build on the culture of the community. One wise decision may be to use parents as resources or adjunct faculty members when possible. This allows outside sources to develop some credibility in the light of other children and especially their own. At all times, school personnel must talk positively about students. If the community or parents perceive that it is a we against them attitude, it is likely that successful change will not take place.

Community Patrons Can Help Too

Within your school district, there are many individuals and community patrons who could assist the school or district in different ways. Some of these strategies follow.

- Establish a graffiti removal campaign.
- Remove block or secretive parties (local student cliques or community gangs).
- Offer parenting classes to help parents gain control of their children.
- Provide recreational and employment opportunities.
- Open schools in evenings to teach parenting, behavior intervention, and courses in English, typing, and so on.
- Establish a gang information system to monitor gang activity.
- Use experts in law enforcement to assist in gang awareness education.
- Do not publish names of gangs when reporting crimes in the media.
- Establish a community-wide educational/awareness program to deal with the gang issue.
- Establish a community gang task force.
- Photograph and report all suspicious groups or persons to law enforcement agencies.
- Establish a school-community advisory council to plan long-term strategies.

The School's Role

By promoting community involvement, the school district is not alone in its mission to create a safe environment. Everyone takes on the responsibility of keeping potential criminal activity from happening. The school should be aware that the proactive approaches that it takes will in the long run become more economical than if it did nothing. There are many positives as a result of the school becoming proactive rather than reactive. Schools and school districts can be the catalyst for developing a positive response to negative student behavior. Some proactive approaches are

- Personal visitations in the community
- Commendation letters to parents
- Truancy and gang hotlines
- Group counseling activities
- Quarterly meetings with parents of gang members
- Parent visitation on a regular basis
- Parent training program
- School-within-a-school (behavior modification, parent/child, etc.)
- School attendance communications to staff and community
- General newsletter in several languages
- Improved inservice activities for staff relating to "at risk" philosophy:
  - Cultural issues
  - Gang styles
  - Substance abuse
  - Community relations
- Student of the month (attendance) award
- Community resources (rewards)
- Other reward programs as deemed appropriate
- Mechanized system of attendance keeping
- School Attendance Review Boards (SARBs)

These approaches are not meant to be exhaustive but a beginning for school districts and buildings to make their own plans. Without some proactive leadership on the part of the administration, nothing will probably happen. And if something does, it will probably be reactive, in which case the school or district is put in a defense posture, which is not conducive to good, positive school-parent-community relations. The moral of this story is to be proactive and ahead of the game, not reactive and a possible loser in the lives of children.

Getting the Community Involved

Administrators who are in crisis situations are already well-acquainted with the community they serve. Principals should develop a telephone number exchange or network parents as well as selected community individuals who have shown interest in assisting the school district with volunteer help. A map also should be developed with telephone numbers of each family that has a student(s) in school for quick reference when needed.

Another strategy that could be developed is to hold neighborhood meetings with student family members and interested community individuals. Have block captains, if desired, and distribute "Gang-Free Zone" signs to be put in windows alerting gang members and potential gang members that the community will be watching. These community groups will be able to document activities going on in their area and report sudden changes as well as names, members, addresses of hangouts, license numbers, and so on.

The establishment of a telephone network has also been very valuable and successful in reducing criminal activity in many school communities. Persistent calls to law enforcement, public agencies, landlords, property owners, and merchants have resulted in significant working relationships that have provided positive changes within school communities. With the help of law enforcement agencies, crime prevention and gang units have been established, and they have worked. These individuals can be invited to meetings to discuss what works and what doesn't. The development of a crime/gang hotline has been very successful in many communities that have experienced recent crime/gang activity. What many communities have experienced is that when a crisis hits, involvement by those affected is the most successful in de-escalating criminal and gang activity.

Organization Is the Key to a Successful Partnership

Being organized is the key to a successful parent-community-school partnership in regard to crisis situations. In regard to criminal or gang activity, this partnership should use pressure points to make sure that those who are prone to participate in such activities are always aware that others are watching. Many criminal activities escalate on rental properties, both high-rise apartments and multiple-family units. Landlords usually do not take on the responsibility to monitor residents. Telephone calls, letters, and petitions to landlords may provide pressure for the landlord to take action. If no action is taken by the landlord, the community can notify city governments of code violations or acts of nuisance, fire hazards, health code violations, and so on.

Many gang and criminal activities are surrounded by drug activities. Public telephones are often used as "drug offices." Pressure to remove these telephone drug offices should be made. If unsuccessful, apply pressure to have outgoing-telephone-calls-only installed. Night lighting is also a successful pressure tactic to discourage gang and criminal activity. Leaving porch lights on is a detractor in many neighborhoods. Also, public buildings in darkened community areas should be pressured to light the outside of their buildings. Sodium vapor/mercury lighting is best for these circumstances.

As was discussed earlier, graffiti cleanup as soon as possible after detection is certainly a detractor. This keeps gang members from gloating over their perceived success. The less notoriety the better in keeping criminal and gang activity in check. The use of neighborhood walks has also been used with some success. This can take some courage if the school community is starting to exert pressure after criminal and gang activity has been in existence for some time. Some caution should be taken with this pressure tactic because personal safety is of primary concern.

A final pressure point could be a letter writing campaign, parents and community members flooding meetings, and local officials visiting schools and school activities. By creating interest in eliminating gangs and criminal activity in schools and local communities, pressure can be applied to sensitive areas where significant results can be generated.

In conclusion, there is no one best way to reduce or eliminate criminal activity in a school or community. It takes a well-organized and well-orchestrated effort by the school, parents, and community to pool their resources and be committed to reduce and possibly eliminate undesirable behavior. Being proactive as a school system enables the school to show leadership and to be an example for acceptable behavior within our society. Most communities and individuals will not know how to tackle such a problem or may believe that becoming involved themselves will have no bearing on the outcome. With the school system as catalyst, a significant impact can be made community-wide as well as schoolwide.

Chapter Eight

Bringing Conflict Management Into the School

In Mrs. Gameon's sixth-grade class, Carla was continually causing trouble and fighting with other students. Students and parents alike were complaining about Carla's behavior both in the classroom and on the playground. Jessica, another sixth-grade student, had enough of Carla's antics and confronted her in the washroom on Thursday afternoon. The discussion escalated to a shouting match that the entire second floor of the school could hear. Within a few seconds, a fight involving Jessica and Carla erupted with both girls drawing blood and two other students and three teachers becoming involved before the fight was broken up.

As the administrator in charge of discipline with little success in using the discipline policy to deter problems, what alternatives might you consider other than an automatic suspension or after-school detentions?

Conflict is not inherently positive or negative. Rather, it is a natural part of life. Conflict affects us all—at all ages, in all settings, within a culture or community, and across cultures and communities. Learning how to look at conflict, how to understand and analyze it, can help us shape more effective and productive responses to it.

Conflict has many definitions. A more abstract definition of conflict is "a state of disharmony" (*Webster's New Collegiate Dictionary*). Hocker and Wilmont (1991) define conflict as "an expressed struggle between at least two interdependent parties who perceive incompatible goals" (p. 83). It is important to note that the differences among beliefs, ideas, opinions,

Understanding Conflict in an Educational Sense

and customs may or may not lead to conflict depending on how, where, and when the differences are behaviorally manifested. Neither of the foregoing definitions denote conflict as either positive or negative. For many of us, however, the connotations of disharmony, incompatibility, and struggle are negative. Our personal associations with the term *conflict* tend to reflect experiences and to reveal assumptions of a conflict as negative, as something to be avoided, if not eliminated. Personal associations are also often emotional. Conflict means anger, hate, betrayal, and loss.

Moving to an understanding of conflict as a neutral phenomenon and as a potentially positive occurrence is critical to improving responses to conflict. Serious problems often arise not from the conflict itself but from responses to it. Thus, understanding conflict is a first step toward productive conflict resolution.

Our feelings, thoughts, physical reactions, and behaviors around conflict stem, at least in part, from the beliefs, assumptions, and experiences with which we were raised. Knowing that conflict is normal and potentially beneficial is not enough to change lifelong beliefs that conflict is dangerous or to alter a patterned response of avoidance.

The field of conflict resolution offers a variety of lenses through which to view conflict. These lenses become tools for learning to step out of old beliefs, ideas, and habits and to see with new eyes. They can assist in obtaining a wider view, in bringing the conflict into sharper focus, and in achieving a more distant perspective. Awareness of different ways of viewing a conflict can keep us from becoming locked into a single, unproductive view.

In addition to learning ways of looking at conflict, we must accept the notion that conflict is everywhere. It exists at all ages, in all settings, in all cultures. Research on conflict with children as young as age 2 shows patterns of conflict similar to what adults experience. Children's conflicts become more complex as they mature, and the proportion of possession conflicts declines over time. In general, however, children's conflicts follow the same general pattern as adult conflicts: They originate, have events and reactions, and finally resolve. Children have needs, interests, and positions, and as they mature, they move from being able to act on or state a position to being able to identify their interests.

Primary developmental tasks of young children include learning problem solving and social cooperation. Children need help learning how to recognize, respond to, and solve the variety of conflicts and problems they encounter. Conflict resolution skills fit within developmentally appropriate curricula for toddlers and preschoolers, and elementary and secondary students.

Conflict is part of the hidden curriculum in all our educational institutions. It exists in classrooms, lunchrooms, teachers' lounges, in the principal's office, in hallways, and on the playgrounds. It exists in college and university faculty meetings, in seminars and labs and dorms. It is a primary fact of life and a constant learning opportunity. Taking charge of what kind of learning occurs from the conflicts that arise is an important and crucial responsibility of all educators.

In an increasingly multicultural society, more and more conflicts arise around cultural, social, and economic life. We must face the differences between cultures without fear and with respect. At the same time, we must recognize that there are no simple answers, in terms of right and wrong, when cultural norms and values clash. In the absence of generalized answers, conflict resolution offers processes for reflection and dialogue that are essential to cross-cultural understanding and dialogue.

Conflict surrounds us and offers rich opportunities for learning about ourselves—our culture, values, needs, and interests—and others—their culture, values, needs, and interests. Unfortunately, most of us view conflict with trepidation, if not fear. The field of conflict resolution offers a variety of tools for stepping back from a conflict and examining it more objectively. What are the characteristics of those involved, the source and type of conflict, the beliefs and stances of those involved? These questions enable us to awaken our curiosity and to see a conflict, whether we are directly involved or merely observing, more fully and to bring to our observations a broader set of knowledge and experience.

As we look at conflicts to gain perspective, understanding, insight, and clarity, we must look at the origins. Who are the parties involved in this conflict, and how can they be characterized? Is the conflict between two individuals, within one person, or is it between two groups or within one group? Is the conflict characterized as intrapersonal or interpersonal? Also, one must look at the cultures of the parties involved, such things as race, ethnicity, gender, religion, socioeconomic status, sexual orientation, occupation, age, and geographic region. As we look at the origins of the conflict, many times questions are answered but the solution still remains unresolved.

A second perspective is gained by looking at the sources of conflict. In other words, what is the conflict about? How can it be generally described? What are some basic sources of conflict? The first two questions are rather easy to get information about. Identifying what the conflict is about and the description of what is happening is generally observational and factual. However, when we look at the third question—What are some basic sources of conflict?—information begins to be less prevalent. Problem solvers need to break the sources of the conflict down into subcategories, such as territory, possessions, control, or access to something or someone, to identify what is actually happening.

As subcategories are identified, one can begin to have an understanding of conflict and look for resolution possibilities. Moore (1986) described five groups of conflicts. These centered around relationships, values, data, interest, and structure. Wall (1985) identified three other groups: interdependence, differences in goals, and differences in perceptions. As we further subdivide our conflict categories, our understanding and perspective change, and we can talk about conflict in terms of categories, instead of the details of the story.

Ask These Questions When Looking at Conflict Types

What type of conflict is this in terms of where movement toward resolution is most likely to occur? What is the potential for resolution? When trying to identify the type of conflict, you may want to ask these questions:

Is the conflict based solely or largely on a misperception or misunderstanding?

Such conflicts are often easily resolved by improved communication.

Does the conflict exist objectively, in fixed conditions?

Ease of resolution depends on the ease of changing conditions. If conditions are rigidly in place, resolution is more difficult.

Is the conflict dependent on conditions that can be easily changed?

If the answer is yes, the conflict may be necessary, but easily remedied through changing external circumstances.

Is the expressed conflict really the central conflict?

If not, resolution is unlikely to be achieved. You need to know what the real conflict is about to see where movement might occur.

Is the conflict being expressed between the right parties?

If not, again, the resolution is difficult. Finding where movement toward resolution can happen most likely depends on having the right people involved.

Is the real conflict submerged, not yet occurring?

A small conflict may signal the beginning of a change in awareness or values that may lead to a much larger conflict later. A conflict over household chores, for example, may be just about household chores, it might be a displaced conflict really about a forgotten anniversary, or it might be the beginning of a much larger change of consciousness about gender roles.

What About Resolution?

In this discussion about conflict resolution, we have looked at the origins, sources, and types of conflict. If conflict is to be resolved, we need to look at beliefs about resolution and what the parties are really trying to accomplish. As for beliefs, the conflict mediator needs to answer the question, What do the parties believe can happen? There are basically three resolutions: Everybody wins or everybody loses, one side wins and one side loses, or everybody must compromise. How we view the potential resolution of conflicts is based on our beliefs and attitudes about relationships, the strength of our focus on goals, our personal characteristics, and past experiences. Also, our comfort with assertiveness and aggression; our cultural norms, values, and expectations; and the cultural setting in which the conflict occurs play a part.

In regard to the question, What are the parties really trying to satisfy? we must also ask, How can we characterize what they really want? In other words, we need to look at their stance on the issue. The conflict mediator needs to resolve these questions: Are the parties taking positions? Are the parties identifying their interests? Are the parties acknowledging their needs? Are the parties aware of the cultural factors influencing their expression of positions, interests, or needs? The mediator must look at all these questions to again focus resolution possibilities. Let's look at each question and determine what the mediator needs to find out.

Are the parties taking positions?

Focus on a specific, concrete outcome(s).

Are the parties identifying their interests?

Focus on the broader goals that each side is trying to achieve. Positions represent one interpretation of how the goal could be met.

Are the parties acknowledging their needs?

Focus on the underlying drive that needs to be met. Interests sit within the context of needs.

Are the parties aware of the cultural factors influencing their expression of positions, interests, or needs?

Focus on the cultural norms and expectations to understand differences.

Finally, the mediator needs to ask, What contributes to achieving a satisfying resolution? There are basically four areas that contribute to resolutions. The people involved understand that underlying needs must be addressed and that in doing this, everyone's interests are going to be explored. Positions individuals take are distinguishable from the interests they have. Their interests are defined and not assumed so that the interests, rather than positions, are the focus for discussion. And finally, conflicting interests are seen as both a shared problem to be solved and cultural differences that should be recognized and understood.

Implementing a Conflict Resolution Program in Your School

Now that we have had a discussion on how to look at conflict and have a clearer understanding of conflict, how can educational administrators implement a conflict resolution program in their school or district? There are many ways, and I will attempt to assist you in developing your vision for what is best for your situation.

Colman McCarty (1992b), a columnist for the *Washington Post* and founder of the Center for Teaching Peace, is also a teacher of a conflict resolution course in a high school in the Washington, D.C., area. He eloquently elucidated how essential it is to teach conflict resolution in schools:

> Studying peace through nonviolence is as much about getting the bombs out of our hearts as it is about getting them out of the Pentagon budget. Every problem we have, every conflict, whether among our family or friends, or among governments, will be addressed either through violent force or nonviolent force. No third option exists. I teach my classes because I believe in nonviolent force—the force of justice, the force of love, the force of sharing wealth, the force of ideas, the force of organized resistance to corrupt power. (p. 24)

McCarty (1992a) further proposed, in a *Washington Post* editorial, that at present it is impossible to deal with conflicts (in schools or anywhere else) dealt with through negotiation, compromise, or other nonviolent means, because those methods have never been consistently taught in school. "We don't know," he says, "because we weren't taught." The result of this academic neglect is "peace illiteracy . . . a land awash in violence." McCarty has proposed that the present federal administration establish a federal Office of Peace Education, which could serve as a resource center for schools.

It appears that individual schools and school districts will need to handle the training of conflict resolution mediators and fend for themselves in resolving local conflicts that arise on their own campuses across this country. As each school or district deals with this concern, the overriding issue should be the focal point in making your decision. Each child deserves the right to attend school in a peaceable classroom environment where he or she is free to learn without harassment, danger of personal bodily harm, or malicious acknowledgments or advances. Kreidler (1984) defined the peaceable classroom where he presented five qualities:

1. *Cooperation.* Children learn to work together and trust, help, and share with each other.
2. *Communication.* Children learn to observe carefully, communicate accurately, and listen sensitively.
3. *Tolerance.* Children learn to respect and appreciate people's differences and to understand prejudice and how it works.

4. *Positive emotional expression.* Children learn to express feelings, particularly anger and frustration, in ways that are not aggressive or destructive, and children learn self-control.
5. *Conflict resolution.* Children learn the skills of responding creatively to conflict in the context of a supportive, caring community. (p. 75)

Bodine, Crawford, and Schrumpf (1994), in their book *Creating a Peaceable School*, built on Kreidler's definition, describing a vision of a peaceable school where two important goals exist:

> First, the school becomes a more peaceful and productive environment where students and teachers together can focus on the real business of learning and having fun. Second, students and adults gain essential life skills that will benefit them not just in school, but also at home, in their neighborhood, and in their roles, present and future, as citizens in a democratic society. (p. 184)

> The defined peaceful environment is one that is based on a philosophy that teaches nonviolence, compassion, trust, fairness, cooperation, respect, and tolerance.

> The pervasive theme in a peaceable school, touching interactions between children, between children and adults, and between adults, is the valuing of human dignity and self-esteem. To build such a foundation in the school . . . all individuals must understand their human rights, respect those rights for self and others, and learn how to exercise their rights without infringing on the rights of others. (Bodine et al., 1994, p. 184)

Building That Peaceable School

A comprehensive orientation toward conflict resolution in schools includes not only questions of classroom method and curriculum content but also issues of whole-school climate and culture. A comprehensive approach to conflict resolution in schools, that is, one that will affect culture and climate as well as academic achievement and individual behavior, includes programming that influences all members of the school family.

As one looks at possibilities for developing a peaceable school or district, the conflict managers program comes to mind. What is the conflict managers program? This is a program that can be developed at either the elementary or secondary level. Conflict managers are specially chosen and trained students who help other students get along with each other. What do conflict managers do? When students are involved in a nonphysical dispute, they are asked if they would like conflict managers to help them solve their problem. If the disputants so choose, the conflict managers help them by using a problem-solving process to clarify the nature of the dispute and to reach a solution satisfactory to both disputants.

Students who are chosen to be conflict managers enter a period of training. This training should be centered around concepts of leadership and communication. Skills to be developed center around how to express feelings and needs as well as how to listen well without taking sides. The art of problem solving is also internalized, with different strategies learned and mastered. Conflict managers learn how to improve the school environment and what it takes to have a peaceable school. Finally, these students learn why and how to take responsibility for their own actions.

Students and adults who complete this training benefit not only by helping to improve the climate and environment within their school or district but also by gaining confidence in their ability to help themselves. Additional benefits include learning to get along better at home and at school. Students who have been trained as conflict managers often improve their grades as well as become models for other students to learn how to get along with each other better. The ultimate benefit is that arguments decrease, so students spend more time learning. Students and teachers are able to work together in a more friendly, relaxed way.

Establishing a Conflict Managers Program

If your school or district is interested in developing a program that has these benefits, then you first need to examine your current school environment. An examination would include the level of tension that exists, the kind and number of student conflicts, the ways conflicts are handled, and the effectiveness of the current approach. If after evaluating this information you have a sense that there is a problem, you may want to learn more about implementing a conflict managers program.

By pursuing the conflict managers program, you should create objectives for the program. Some examples might be the following:

- To decrease tension, hostility, conflict, and violence in school
- To enable students to build cooperation with other students, parents, and teachers
- To teach students communication, problem-solving, and conflict resolution skills
- To enable students to exercise responsibility for improving their school environment

On completion of your objectives, students should be selected for the program. It is advised that students be elected by classmates and teachers based on their leadership skills and potential. Each student will be trained in interpersonal communication and conflict resolution skills. After training, the students work in pairs to help other students resolve their conflicts using a specific problem-solving process. Students have biweekly meetings with the faculty coordinator to discuss problems, share experiences, receive additional training, and resolve issues.

As a school or district is developing its program for implementation, a minimum of two staff members must be selected to act as trainers/coordinators for the program. These teachers should be released from classroom responsibilities for 4 to 8 hours two times per year to serve as trainers. Within the teachers' training, they must be educated about the program and convinced that it will work. Teachers and administrators must be willing to release students from classes to attend training, when they are on duty, and to attend biweekly meetings. Students should be required to make up any work missed.

As the school or district develops and works toward implementation of this type of program, it is imperative that the board of education or board of directors be advised as to the objectives and intent of the program. It is wise to be proactive and anticipate board and community reaction to the implementation of such a program. Remember, some will think you are wasting your time, whereas others will herald your initiative. Wisdom without implementation is merely an academic exercise; implementation of a program without wisdom and foresight is professional suicide. Wisdom, foresight, and implementation can change your school or district into a smooth-running, educationally sound and safe environment.

Student Assistance Team

Another approach a school or district may take is to develop a student assistance program. This type of program goes beyond the conflict managers program discussed previously and involves additional resources within the school/district and community. Many of the student assistance program functions are preventive as well as corrective. Student incidence could range greater than the conflict mode discussed earlier. See Chapter 6 for a full description of the student assistance program.

Chapter Nine

Being Proactive in Dealing With Gangs

Tuesday afternoon, Principal Jonikaitis received a telephone call from a parent of one of his middle school students complaining of the harassment that his son was receiving from a group of boys during lunch and after school. Principal Jonikaitis had been alerted once before about this group's behavior and had started to watch the group more closely. On further observation, he noticed the boys were all wearing the same color shirts and the same color shoelaces in their shoes. Prinicipal Jonikaitis thought this was somewhat odd and started to ask some questions of other faculty members and community members including the local police department.

What type of questions would you ask? Where in your community could you get the answers to your questions? When you get your answers and it appears that there is a problem or potential problem, what are you going to do?

Children who are entering schools today have some unique problems or concerns that administrators, teachers, staff, and community members will have to deal with and resolve if these children are going to have a productive place in our society. Children are born today with drug-addiction symptoms; many children are abused, unloved; children are born into dysfunctional families and families with either one or no parents. Concerns of educators in the 1960s centered around such things as cutting in line, chewing gum, running in the halls, talking out of turn, and littering. How times have changed! Concerns of educators in the 1990s center around assaults, gangs and gang fights, robberies, drug and alcohol abuse, and drive-by shootings.

Gangs Are Not Only an Urban Problem

Today, in many communities across this country there are developing gangs and groups of students who are banding together for singular or multiple purposes with intent to disrupt communities, schools, or neighborhoods. To discuss gangs and gang behavior, we first need a definition of a gang. A *gang* is a group of three or more persons who meet on a regular basis, have a common group name, have defined leadership, have common signs or dress (colors), have an area of operation (turf), and collectively engage in criminal activity.

In many communities and neighborhoods today, children are being pressured to behave in ways that are acceptable to their peers. If there is gang activity, that means behavior that could lead to disastrous consequences for the child. As administrators, teachers, staff, and community, it does take a "community to raise a child." Observable behavior should be the first indication that a child is becoming involved in a potential dangerous situation.

As students become acquainted and interested in gangs, what is known as pregang behavior can develop. Such behavior usually results in starting to have poor academic progress, if that has not been the case previously. Students start to become truant from school or not attend all of their classes as well as becoming resentful of authority. They start to have negative police contact and start to dress in traditional gang attire. They appear to have an interest in and identify with martial arts or similar forms of combative behavior. Usually, students who live in "high-risk" neighborhoods or communities that have high unemployment, large transient populations, large ethnic communities, or little or no recreational facilities run a higher risk of becoming involved with gangs. As these gangs and gang activities become commonplace, and well documented and publicized, there appears to be a segment of the student population that are called "wanna-bes," those students who are looking for acceptance by a peer group and who try to model some behavior that they believe will be acceptable to a portion of the student population in either the school or the community.

Schools as Enablers

As school administrators and educators, we sometimes become enablers of gang behavior. Many schools are interested only in teaching and having learning experiences. Hence, some schools lose sight of what is happening to their students. Schools that have had problems with gangs and gang behavior or schools that are becoming involved with gangs and gang behavior usually have students who have negative expectations about themselves, the community, and the school environment. Many times, faculty and staff become pessimistic about students, and students feel and believe that no one cares. Many times, schools do not have sufficient policies dealing with discipline or the students' perception of discipline is that committing the negative act is worth the disciplinary action. Another enabler that students understand is when the school has a separatist attitude between the school and home. If students know that there will be very little, if any, contact or communication with the home, they feel more confident in doing whatever they want to do without being chastised or disciplined for their actions.

Gang behavior becomes more apparent when there is a large measure of insensitivity to racial and/or ethnic concerns. Students band together when they believe they are being taken advantage of or mistreated. Rebellion often comes after a segment of the population believes that it has been the victim of some form of mistreatment.

As teachers and staff members start to become frustrated with existing conditions or when once-good working conditions have deteriorated to a point where they are now saying, "This used to be a nice place," an attitude of "I don't care anymore" will pervade. This will only add fuel to the gang behavior as gangs will believe that they have the situation well in hand. Along with this attitude problem, if the administration continually denies that a problem exists and does not seek outside help, such as the local law enforcement agency, or fails to communicate within the school as well as to the community at large, gang behavior will flourish. Awareness, communication, and concern on the part of administrators, faculty and staff, parents, and community members will assist in reducing gang behavior.

Finally, schools need to look at the types of activities that are offered to students. See if there are any uninspiring activities that are not attracting students. Many programs have a tendency to exclude students or welcome only those who are gifted or talented. Many successful programs have revised their school activities to include all segments of the student population and offer those activities after school and well into the late evening.

How Gangs Evolve

Gangs and gang behavior evolve from many different societal situations and environmental conditions. Figure 9.1 illustrates the many types of gangs that could be functioning in your school or community. Many people believe that the only type of gangs are those known as "street gangs." In contrast, there are many more types that are formed due to some societal connection or environmental condition in which students/children find themselves becoming participants.

Gang Clothing and Other Markings (Symbols)

Just as there are many different types of gangs, there are many different types of gang symbols that give membership identification to a particular group. Figure 9.2 identifies some gang clothing. As a school administrator, you need to be cognizant of such symbols or clothing for future reference and identification. These symbols range from baseball hats to wearing bandannas, specific shirts/jackets/overcoats, and a certain kind of pants or shoes. Some symbols may even take the form of tattoos/burns,

Social gangs	Mostly engage in drug and alcohol abuse. First step to criminal street gang.
Criminal street gangs	Engage mostly in property crimes: auto theft, burglary, graffiti, assaults. Next step to violent street gang.
Violent street gangs	Engage in violent crime: murder, aggravated assault, kidnapping, drive-by shootings.
Racist gangs	Engage in assault on ethnic groups. Hate crimes based on race or sexual orientation. "Skinheads."
Asian gangs	Engage in extortion, robbery, drug and gun running, money laundering. Low-key, hard to identify. Hard-core members are very violent.
Prison gangs	Influence gang activity outside of the prison. Engage in drug and gun running, use youth gangs to commit many types of criminal activity. Very violent.

Figure 9.1. Types of Gangs

jewelry, or hairstyles. Many gangs have access to pagers and cellular telephones, have hand signs that denote their membership and participation in the gang, or both.

Gang clothing or identification marking is a significant contribution to gang participation. It symbolizes group acceptance and brings members together for whatever cause or direction. Gang clothing or markings may also signify a geographical area or turf the gang has staked out or believes it controls. This turf has significant ramifications for nonmembers or rival gang members: The general understanding for nongang members is "stay out."

Gang Mythology

For gang-suppression strategies to work effectively, common myths about gangs needs to be dispelled. All concerned need to be informed about the realities of gangs and gang mentality. The following list of gang myths was furnished by Lorne Krammer, chief of police in Colorado Springs, Colorado.[1]

Myth 1—The majority of street gang members are juveniles. Juveniles—those who are 18 years or younger—actually comprise a minority of gang membership. In Los Angeles County, juveniles represent only about 20% of gang members. Across the nation, the tenure of gang membership is increasing from as early as 9 to 10 years. Money, drugs, and lax juvenile laws are each key factors in this transition to attracting kids to gangs at younger ages.

Baseball hats	Sports team logo Gang logo Worn backward Worn sideways
Bandannas	Colors—rags Denote color of gang
Shirts, jackets, or overcoats	Gang name Monikers Colors Style—work Work shirts—Dickies Pendletons Sports teams—color most important
Pants	Jeans, work pants, or uniform Baggy, no belt Hanging on hips
Shoes	Color important Shoelaces with gang color Brand names, for example, British Knights: Blood Killers Doc Martens boots (hate groups) Nazi-style boots
Tattoos and/or burns	Tattoos of gang name and street name Tattoo of animal or dragon All gang members have same tattoo Teardrop under eye—for fallen member Spider-web next to thumb Burns on back of hands or arm—gang initiation
Jewelry and other	Heavy gold chain with firearms Hair net Beaded necklaces with gang colors Pagers and cellular telephones Hand signs
Hairstyles	All members wear the same hairstyle. Look for same hairstyle on suspected gang member.

Figure 9.2. Gang Clothing and Other Markings

Myth 2—All street gangs are turf oriented. Some gangs may not claim any specific turf, whereas other gangs may operate in multiple locations or even in very unsuspecting small cities. One Asian gang that operated crime rings from Florida to California had its headquarters in a small Pennsylvania town of fewer than 4,500 residents.

Myth 3—Females are not allowed to join gangs. Females are joining gangs in record numbers and often are extremely violent. In times past, females were thought of simply as "mules"—transporters of weapons or drugs—or as innocent bystanders. Females now make up about 5% of gang members, and this number is increasing.

Myth 4—Gang weapons usually consist of chains, knives, and tire irons. Perhaps brass knuckles, knives, and chains were the key weapons in the gangs of yesteryear, but today Uzis, AK-47s, and other semiautomatics are the weapons of choice.

Myth 5—All gangs have one leader and are tightly structured. Most gangs are loosely knit groups and likely will have several leaders. If one member is killed, other potential gang leaders seem to be waiting in the wings.

Myth 6—Graffiti is merely an art form. Graffiti is much more than an art form. It is a message that proclaims the presence of the gang and offers a challenge to rivals. Graffiti serves as a form of intimidation and control—an instrument for advertising.

Myth 7—One way to cure gang membership is by locking the gang member(s) away. Incarceration and rehabilitation of hard-core gang members have not proven effective. Changing criminal behavior patterns is difficult. Prisons often serve as command centers and institutions of "higher learning" for ongoing gang-related crime. Often, prisoners are forced to take sides with one group or another simply for protection.

Myth 8—Gangs are a law enforcement problem. Gangs are a problem for everyone. Communities need to develop systemwide programs to effectively address gang problems in their areas. Not merely a school problem, gangs are a community problem and a national challenge. Responding to gangs requires a systematic, comprehensive, and collaborative approach that incorporates prevention, intervention, and suppression strategies. Whereas each strategy has a specific vision and pressing mandate, the greatest hope is on prevention, for only by keeping children from joining gangs in the first place will we be able to halt the rising tide of terror and violence that gangs represent.

Take the Gang Assessment Survey

Figure 9.3 is the Gang Assessment Tool, which will help determine the presence of gangs on school campuses. This requires an awareness of the complex issues that evolve into gang membership, a readiness to be prepared "just in case," and a decisive pledge to actively protect the interest of the majority—those who want an education in a secure environment. Often, a school administrator will not recognize the preliminary signs of gang activity. Some see admission of gang presence as a personal failing rather than a community problem.

Each yes answer will score the number of points following the question.

Do you have graffiti on or near your campus? (5)

Do you have crossed-out graffiti on or near your campus? (10)

Do your students wear colors, jewelry, clothing; flash hand signals; or display other behavior that may be gang related? (10)

Are drugs available near your school? (5)

Has there been a significant increase in the number of physical confrontations/stare-downs within the past 12 months in or around your school? (5)

Is there an increasing presence of weapons in your community? (10)

Are beepers, pagers, or cellular telephones used by your students? (10)

Have you had a drive-by shooting at or around your school? (15)

Have you had a "show-by" display of weapons at or around your school? (10)

Is the truancy rate of your school increasing? (5)

Are there increasing numbers of racial incidents occurring in your community or school? (5)

Is there a history of gangs in your community? (10)

Is there an increasing presence of "informal social groups" with unusual names, like the "Woodland Heights Posse," "Rip Off and Rule," "Females Simply Chillin," or "Kappa Phi Nasty"? (15)

Point values should be totaled. The following scores will indicate the level of need for a school security review: 0-15 points, no significant gang problem; 20-40 points, an emerging gang problem; 45-60 points, a significant gang problem for which a gang prevention and gang intervention plan should be developed; 65 points or higher, an acute gang problem that merits a total gang prevention intervention and suppression program.

Figure 9.3. Gang Assessment Tool
SOURCE: National School Safety Center.

The National School Safety Center has developed the Gang Assessment Tool to help communities overcome the problem of denial and to determine the extent of gang and gang-related activity in the vicinity of the school. The first step in confronting a problem like gang activity is to recognize that there is (or are) gang(s) in the community. Some form of action plan needs to be developed to protect individuals who do not want to belong to such organizations as well as to involve the community and community agencies to help minimize the impact of such organizations. Denial by administrators of such organizations or activity in the community or in school puts the entire student population at risk.

Levels of Gang Activity	Gang Prevention/Intervention Process
1. No known gang activity 　Have some existing gang prevention and education programs 　Recreation, employment, and other programs for youth 　Strong sense of community/family 　Minimum crime/delinquency	Maintain existing programs/priority Reinforce positive attitudes for family, home, community, and laws Maintain strong business/civic interaction
2. Limited gang activity 　Gangs near your community; sporadic gang crimes/graffiti 　Limited gang intrusion 　General indifference/denial 　Community passive/"let others respond"	Share gang intelligence and program information School and community prevention/education programs Increase sports and other community activities Graffiti abatement efforts Antigang information campaign
3. Emerging gang activity 　One or more gangs in area 　Local schools and parks are hangouts 　Loss of community identity/pride 　Limited short-term countermeasures 　Increase in gang crimes	Develop and implement target area strategies Specialized gang suppression/abatement Community mobilization ("Reclaim the Community") Parent education/accountability Job placement (youth at risk)
4. Community in crisis 　Major gang activity/drive-bys 　Parks and schools dominated by gangs 　Community living in fear 　Increase in truancy, dropouts, and crime 　Police overburdened	Develop and implement major community mobilization efforts Collaboration among community groups, antigang professionals, law enforcement "Reclaim the Schools, Parks, Kids" campaign
5. Gang-controlled community 　Gangs dominate most of daily life 　Tax base eroded/businesses flee 　An illegal economy thrives 　General breakdown of family/community 　Institutional response to gangs overwhelmed	Declare gang "state of emergency" Majority of efforts left to professionals Develop a block-by-block effort Selected resident/law enforcement patrols

Figure 9.4. Gang Assessment and Planning Guide

Gang Assessment and Planning Guide

As part of the evaluation of the present condition in a school or community, there will be a need to develop a planning guide for the level of activity that you find in your school or community. Figure 9.4 will help you develop the next step in the prevention/intervention process. It will assist in what should be happening given the level of gang activity. The

Planning Process	Comprehensiveness	Program Strategies
Sound planning	Target multiples	Information and education
Common vision	Multiple systems	Life skills
Assessment of needs and resources	Whole community	Alternatives
Goal setting	All youth	Social policy
Task sequencing	Health promotion	Training impactors
Responsibility	Long-term duration	Early-intervention systems
Management	Adequate quantity	
Evaluation	Integration with other activities	
Replanning		
Collaboration		
Measurable goals		

Figure 9.5. Characteristics of Effective Prevention Programs

need to be proactive at this stage is critical and crucial to the success that a school or community may have in the future. One thing is for sure, if nothing is done, the situation will become a major problem and even possibly a "fatal error" for some students.

Characteristics of a Successful Prevention Program

Figure 9.5 addresses the characteristics of effective prevention programs. Understanding the planning process and the comprehensiveness and development of program strategies will enable the school administrator to stay on top of the issue and be proactive in developing the leadership that is needed in times of emotion and distress. While maintaining a proactive and catalystic approach to gang prevention/intervention, there is a need to establish high visibility with staff as well as making them conscious of the activity surrounding them. Everyone involved will become graffiti conscious and become more perceptive of possibilities that could happen on school grounds or within the community. With a proactive approach and involving the faculty and staff, members of the gang community can be identified, and everyone involved can be observing, not just the administrator. There is an old saying that "a thousand eyes are better than two."

Some other proactive approach ideas that can be useful are to

- Be prepared to enforce all rules
- Treat all rumors as truth
- Include gang members in problem-solving activities—as individuals
- Include gang members in school projects, especially during ethnic holidays

- Maintain positive relationships with local law enforcement
- Establish a parents-as-partners attitude, which encourages visitations, and to develop a parent phone tree

Recommendations for Parents and Educators

Figures 9.6, 9.7, and 9.8 serve as recommendations for educators and, more specifically, counselors and parents, to assist them as they work with students who are either gang members or wanna-be gang members. As gangs evolve and develop, many questions will be asked and common cries will be heard: What should I do? If I only knew who to talk to! These recommendations can help the administrator and others as they confront and tackle one of the biggest problems they will ever face.

Recommendations for educators, counselors, and parents are needed as a plan in being prepared. There is also a need to reinforce the concept of a safe school environment and how that interacts with the effective schools movement. Administrators should not get caught up in only addressing gang activity. Because administrators are looked to for establishing and maintaining a safe learning environment, they need to make sure that other areas of school safety are addressed as well.

Areas of Concern Related to Gangs and Safe Schools

An administrator needs to address the following areas. The attitude that school is "fine" and that there is no problem, when there is a problem, is denial. Remember, gang activity is not the administrator's personal problem nor does it reflect on his or her ability as an administrator. It is a community and societal problem that takes a "we" attitude to help in the prevention/intervention process. When an administrator disciplines at all costs and the discipline is based on fear and intimidation, a climate of uncertainty and resentment is created. This will not establish a learning environment but will escalate a negative situation. Developing a discipline policy that addresses particular situations with education rather than determent may have a lasting effect on those who reap the "wrath" of discipline. Discipline policies that have been well thought-out and communicated to students, parents, and the community will go a long way in addressing and communicating the problem. For instance, allowing gang attire and foul language to continue in school without some consequences breeds conditions for an unsafe school. Inattention and insensitivity to ethnic or racial concerns will always provide an unsafe condition. Finally, peer pressure situations that are allowed to exist, poorly articulated policies, lack of consistent enforcement, and ineffective follow-through are all conditions that are apparent in unsafe schools when gangs and gang activity are involved.

1. Establish and enforce clear codes of school conduct that stress the unacceptability of gang behavior.
2. Remove graffiti as soon as possible. If the vandals are known, involve them in the cleanup. If possible, take photographs before removal for graffiti file. Report the crime to the local law enforcement agency and take school disciplinary action.
3. Learn to identify groups on campus responsible for graffiti, as well as their nicknames and style of graffiti. Call them to a conference to discuss campus pride and ways to eliminate graffiti at school.
4. Eliminate gang intimidation of students.
5. Eliminate on-campus confrontations between members of different gangs.
6. Assimilate gang-oriented students into the mainstream—academically, extracurricularly, and socially.
7. Be aware of and prepared to deal with gangs.
8. Train your teachers and staff to recognize gangs.
9. Encourage your school district to take a tough stand against gangs. Have them adopt or consider policies to deal with gangs.
10. Involve the community, parents, and the police.
11. Change the thinking habits of younger kids. Redirect their energies away from gangs.
12. Recognize that some of these kids are on different tracks. They do not need to compete with those kids who are planning on going to college.
13. Start prevention in the early grades. Many teachers believe that once kids reach high school and are involved in a gang, they are already "hard core."
14. Create school curriculums that focus on nonviolence, conflict resolution, effective decision making, and gang prevention.
15. Let the gangs and community know you will not allow gangs to control the school.
16. Monitor your school campus for signs of gang activity.
17. Search lockers or students whenever there is an indication of weapons or drugs.
18. Prohibit, on school property or at school-sponsored events, the display of certain clothing or adornments that indicate gang membership.
19. Monitor visitors who come to the school campus.
20. Establish programs that stress positive youth involvement.
21. Have a clear-cut policy in regard to weapons.
22. Provide in-school programs and support groups for students, and their parents, who display characteristics that may lead to gang activity.
23. Emphasize to students that they are actually doing themselves, others, and even the perpetrators a favor by reporting the presence of weapons on campus.

Figure 9.6. Recommendations for Educators *(continued)*

24. Implement drug and alcohol abuse prevention programs in your school.
25. Encourage students to stay in school.
26. If possible, remove paraphernalia from gang members. This includes pagers that are used in narcotics traffic and distinctive clothing that they may wear including jackets, hats, and things that have the name of the gang on it.
27. Make students aware of what being in a gang brings.
28. Investigate any rumors you hear from students about anticipated gang activity.
29. Handle any gang activity on campus immediately.
30. Communicate to students and their parents that gang activity will not be tolerated.
31. Let students know the penalty for vandalism and graffiti offenses.

Figure 9.6. Recommendations for Educators *(continued)*

School Discipline When Gangs or Gang Members Are Involved

When administrators deal with school discipline and gangs are involved, it is better to establish firm, fair policies that reflect an attitude of community unity within the campus. Administrators *must* handle discipline violations independently with each gang member. As the administrator discusses discipline policies and consequences, it is important to discuss the difference between criminal behavior and discipline. It is also wise to discuss the involvement of law enforcement in serious criminal activities. Communicate in no uncertain terms to gang members that they will be held accountable for their action—law violators will be prosecuted. When gangs are just forming in schools or communities, it is important to swiftly chip away at their activity to reduce gang attractiveness for borderline individuals or groups.

The need for a crisis management plan that links the school, the community, and law enforcement agencies together is a beginning to turn the unsafe school into a healthy learning environment for all children. In addition, involving the faculty and allowing them to accept some responsibility and accountability for assisting in establishing a learning environment will be a big step in raising their expectations and ownership.

Most, if not all, administrators have read about or have been a part of the effective schools movement during the past decade. Developing a mission statement, having well-defined goals, and establishing a communication network between school and community are but a few of the tenets that have been researched and addressed as effective schools characteristics. For gang-related and gang-infested environments, other characteristics are needed to bring the school into a safe and effective learning environment. Along with those characteristics mentioned previously, gang-infested schools need to have consistent discipline and attendance policies—no wavering on these issues. Also, effective student

1. Understand gangs, their local characteristics and strengths.
2. Be a good listener.
3. Show students that you care.
4. Do not be afraid to work with them.
5. Find out how involved they are with the gang.
6. Offer them an opportunity to discuss gang membership.
7. Learn to work with members of different gangs and try to reduce hostility between rival gangs.
8. Describe the negative aspects of gang membership.
9. Provide them with alternatives to gang membership.
10. Let them know there is a way out.
11. Make them aware of the impact of gang membership on their family.
12. Understand that a youth will only remain in a gang as long as the gang makes him or her feel powerful and needed. Offer gang members activities that will foster a healthy feeling of self-worth, independence, and responsibility, thus replacing the need for gang membership.
13. Teach them lessons that discourage gang membership and instead propose constructive alternatives.
14. Refer them to work experience and employment opportunities. Healthy diversions are among the most effective alternatives to gang participation.
15. Invite guest speakers who have been involved with gangs or who deal with the consequences of gang behavior, including law enforcers, juvenile court judges, and probation officers.

Figure 9.7. Recommendations for Counselors Working With Students Involved in Gangs

support groups such as peer counseling, crisis counseling, and a student assistance program should be established. Parental involvement in school activities is a necessity. Staff development is a key ingredient for a gang-infested school. Staff development on safe school issues, gang awareness, and violence prevention are just a few areas in which staff members should be trained. In preservice preparation programs across this country, there is very little taught about to gangs, gang activity, and survival techniques when confronted with crime and violence. Are your school and staff ready and able to meet the challenge when, not if, the challenge arrives on your school's doorstep?

Be Proactive in Keeping Your School Safe

Figure 9.9 outlines how a school might take a proactive approach in keeping itself safe. Remember the need to deal with prevention, intervention, and suppression. These are three key areas that need to be addressed if a school is going to be proactive.

Being Proactive in Dealing With Gangs 117

1. Know all about drugs and gangs in your community.
2. Educate yourself about what's happening in your neighborhood.
3. Work to have a good family unit at home because that is what a gang offers.
4. Remove your child from the gang's influence as soon as possible. This might mean asking for the help of your child's school, church, police department, or probation department.
5. Explain to your child what you expect of him or her and the consequences if he or she does not do what you expect.
6. Praise your child for the good things he or she does.
7. Spend time with your child. Do things with your child that he or she enjoys doing.
8. Listen to your child.
9. Love your child. Tell your child that you love him or her.
10. Keep up with how your child is doing in school. Talk to your child's teachers. If your child is falling behind in his or her schoolwork, find someone who can tutor your child.
11. If necessary, move out of your neighborhood. Move your child to another school.
12. Stress to your child the importance of an education.
13. Take an interest in the life of your child.
14. Encourage your child.
15. Be concerned about your child.
16. Ask your child about his or her day at school.
17. Take the time to know your child's friends.

Figure 9.8. Recommendations for Parents

Part of keeping schools safe is also understanding the roles of the participants within the school, specifically, the principal, teacher, and student. Figure 9.10 indicates how each will need to be involved.

Participant Roles in School Safety Planning

A school's staff members need to have high visibility. Establishing a presence is an important part of maintaining a safe environment. The ability to identify student leaders also creates a climate for a positive direction as well as allows the student body to establish some leadership accountability. It is crucial that an administration responds to parent, community, and student concerns. If the perception is that no communication exists or that the administration does not care or is ineffective, a major breakdown will result that ultimately may create a major problem in establishing a safe environment.

Additional Strategies for Establishing a Safe School

Prevention	Violence prevention curriculum and staff training Goal setting and decision making Positive alternatives and activities
Intervention and changing behavior	Peer mediator groups Anger management/control Problem-solving skills Conflict resolution training Motivation/self-esteem programs
Suppression	Strict enforcement of code of conduct and rules Metal detectors Dress code Graffiti removal Identify and track hard-core gang members Zero tolerance for criminal acts Crimestoppers program

Figure 9.9. Keeping Schools Safe

An administrator needs to develop an information network within the school and community. Communication between community agencies and the local law enforcement agency is crucial to keep all informed as to school and community activities. A school safety advisory board, with parent, teacher, student, and law enforcement representatives, can assist the administration and school in developing strategies for continuing a safe school environment. Part of the responsibility of the advisory board could be to publish a school safety/gang awareness brochure to increase parent and community awareness.

When vandalism happens, the school administration needs to be proactive in establishing some form of an incentive program to keep the building and grounds free from vandalism and graffiti. When gang activity is prevalent in such cases, there may be an opportunity to work with these groups in establishing contests, where a positive result could be achieved rather than vandalism. The successful administrator in also one who can identify students by name and nickname. This allows students to feel comfortable with the administrator—his or her style and personality. By knowing the student body, the administrator becomes more aware of nonstudents on campus. When nonstudents are confronted, keep files for possible future reference. Keeping files and records of nonstudent vehicles that constantly appear around the school is important information that may be very useful for future reference. To get this information, the administration needs to work with the student leaders and other students to help identify all nonstudents as well as gang members who may be students. The administration should take a proactive attitude: Tell the campus intruders that the school will be willing to prosecute them as trespassers or for other violations if they can be documented. When intruders enter or gang activity happens in buildings or on school grounds,

Principal	Defines the purpose of the safety plan
	Communicates regularly with the community
	Sets high expectations for staff and students
	Evaluates the safety plan
	Is knowledgeable of current prevention programs
	Encourages positive law enforcement participation
Teacher	Has high visibility
	Reports criminal violations promptly and professionally
	Has clear standards of academic performance and conduct
	Treats all students equally
Student	Contributes to family spirit by participating in student activities
	Identifies gang names and information
	Assists in organizing activities that involve all students
	Takes pride in the school and community

Figure 9.10. Roles in School Safety Planning

the administration needs to be in contact with the local police department, and if graffiti is found in buildings, the administration needs to have it removed as soon as possible. The administration of the school must deal quickly and firmly with students who are causing problems, whether they are nonstudents or gang members.

A final strategy that can have a positive effect, especially if parent involvement is perceived to be positive, is to notify parents of suspected gang membership. Criticism may be forthcoming if an administrator happens to notify a parent whose child is not in a gang, but in those rare cases, it is better to be safe than sorry. Administrators can also argue the point that they had the student's best interest at heart and the information and observation indicated the need to notify the parent(s).

Note

1. This information was provided at an October 19, 1991 meeting in Colorado Springs, Colorado.

Resource A

Crisis Situations and Anticipated Response

Crisis management planning's main purpose is to serve as an aid in the event of a crisis situation. Its goal is to assist school personnel in establishing a network and guidelines for dealing with such areas as shock, grief, and the healing process that follows many crisis situations. Remember, a crisis is an extraordinary event and therefore cannot be predicted. In light of this, administrators need to be prepared to deal with unanticipated, unpredictable, and extraordinary situations. An administrator or administrative team, given time and energy at a nonstressful time, can establish guidelines that assist in times of stress and crisis. With this in mind, the examples are presented as a model for a crisis management plan that can be developed around the specifics of a school or district and a community.

The district must be prepared to respond to a wide range of natural and other emergencies. The manner in which a building or district and a community respond to an emergency can often reduce personnel injuries and/or damage to school property. Planning must be based on the major threats to the safety of the school. Although not every type of emergency can be planned for, the most common situations can be. The examples provide a framework for response to those situations. However, no plan can substitute for good common sense applied at the critical moment.

For the planning process, school administrations need to develop emergency and crisis plans in at least eight areas:

1. Major bus accident during school hours, with injuries
2. Fire or explosion at school, with injuries
3. A train or truck accident requiring immediate evacuation
4. Weather disaster causing injuries and damage
5. Bomb threat to school
6. Kidnapping/terrorist situation
7. Personal crisis situation
8. Weapons and other police emergencies

A school/community-based response plan is critical to the efficient handling of a crisis situation. It is imperative that school personnel become familiar with the guidelines and procedures for handling crisis situations. This also includes effective communication both internally and externally.

Once the crisis management plan has been developed and approved by the board of education or board of directors, each member of the crisis management team and each administrator and board member should have a copy. In addition, every employee of the district should be given a crisis management flip chart that provides procedures and guidelines at a glance.

If finances are available, a brochure should be developed explaining the purposes and basic procedures that parents and community members should follow a crisis situation. The more basic information that can be disseminated, the less confusion and frustration there will be at the crisis point. This will aid the school, administrator, and staff when calmness needs to prevail. By becoming proactive, parents and community members establish a great deal of confidence and trust when difficult situations arise.

It is with this in mind that the following examples are given. I am grateful to the Spring Branch Independent School District and the Eagle Mountain–Saginaw Independent School District, both in the state of Texas, for developing excellent crisis plans and giving permission for their plans to be used as models for other districts. May your school, district, and community never, ever have to use the plans that your district may develop. However, if there is a need to activate a crisis plan, you will, at that time, realize the importance of proactive preparation for such an event.

SAMPLE CRISIS PLANS

(Individual Crisis)

Resource A

Bus Accident With Serious Injury and/or Fatality

It is likely that most bus accidents will occur in close proximity of the school district.

First Actions

- Driver and/or aide remain calm.
- If threat of fire, move children and others to safe location.
- Administer first aid.
- Call for emergency help (police, fire, ambulance, etc.).

Other Actions

- Call Spring Branch Police Department dispatcher (984-****).
- Call Transportation Center (827-****).
    1. Transportation will make call to associate superintendent.
    2. Transportation will notify the Communications Department if circumstances warrant.
- Call principal: _____

    Assistant principal: _____

    Director: _____
- Make no statements to the media. Refer them to civil authorities on site or to the office of the Communications Department (464-**** x 2272 or 2273).

Precautionary Measures

- Follow Board policy and administrative regulation when making field trips.
- Keep important phone numbers in bus for emergency phone calls.

SOURCE: Spring Branch ISD Crisis Management Plan. Used with permission.

Bus and Auto Accidents on Trips Away From District

Precautionary Measures
Before Leaving District

- Check to see if first aid kit and other emergency equipment are on the bus as required by law.

- Take along a list of students in attendance. Include for each a home telephone number, names of parents, parents' work telephone, home address, and any indications of health or medical problems.

- Take along a list of the emergency phone numbers listed below.

- Take along a list of sponsors and teachers who are in attendance on trip, their home addresses and home phone numbers, name and work telephone of spouse or nearest relative, and medical and health information regarding each adult.

- Have more than one copy of the above lists and leave one list with the school principal; perhaps share another list with another sponsor or place a list in a designated location for easy access to other adults on trip (glove/map compartment).

- Follow Board policy and administrative regulation on field trips.

In the event of an accident

- Remain calm.

- If threat of fire exists, move children to a safe place.

- Call emergency vehicles/services: police, fire, ambulance, highway patrol, and begin administration of first aid.

- Call Spring Branch ISD Police Department dispatcher (984-****).

- Call Transportation Department (827-****).

- Call Principal: _____

    Assistant principal: _____

    Director: _____

- Do not issue statements to the press. Refer the press to civil authorities in charge or to the Communications Department (464-**** x 2272 or 2273).

SOURCE: Spring Branch ISD Crisis Management Plan. Used with permission.

Resource A

Accidents and Medical Emergencies

Purpose

All school personnel have a responsibility to prevent accidents and help ensure a safe school environment.

The health services staff in particular is primarily responsible for:

- Coordinating and training of faculty and staff in emergency care
- Preventing accidents by promoting a healthful environment
- Administering cardiopulmonary resuscitation (CPR) and first aid
- Securing adequate emergency care information for each student
- Maintaining comprehensive documentation and reporting of accidents, injuries, and emergencies
- Assisting in setting up shelters and/or emergency aid stations under the direction of the local Red Cross agency (if so directed)

The Health Services Emergency Care System will function in cooperation with the individual school's crisis management plan.

Emergency Care System

- The building principal/building administrator will ensure that an Emergency Care Team will be appointed and will be prepared to act in a prompt, efficient, and effective manner. The nurse and/or nurse assistant will function as the coordinator of this team and will keep all members advised of current procedures. This team should have at least one member in addition to the nurse or nurse assistant who is qualified in cardiopulmonary resuscitation (CPR).

- Health services staff will maintain an adequate inventory of clinical/medical/first aid supplies and ensure that all staff have received appropriate training in district infectious disease procedures.

- A current and complete Emergency Telephone Roster, including listings for the Poison Control Center and other agencies, should be posted in the clinic.

SOURCE: Eagle Mountain–Saginaw Independent School District Crisis Management Plan. Used with permission.

Accidents To and From School

In the event of accidents involving an employee or child who is on the way to or from school, try to determine whether or not help is on the way.

If help is not on the way, these are actions to consider:

- Call police (911) as indicated by nature of accident.
- Call Fire Department ambulance (911), or other ambulance, as indicated by nature of accident.
- Call Boswell Liaison Officer (237-****), Tarrant County Sheriff's Department (884-****), Saginaw Police Department (232-****), and/or Blue Mound Police Department (232-****).
- Discuss situation with an associate at place of parent's or guardian's employment, or spouse's or relative's place of employment when parent, spouse, or relative is unavailable.

If help is on the way, these are actions to consider:

- If not reached earlier, continue to try to notify parents, spouse, or closest neighbor or relative.
- If parents, spouse, or closest relative are unavailable, discuss situation with an associate at the place of employment or the parents, guardian, spouse, or closest relative.
- Send a trusted employee to observe the situation.
- Calls may be referred to civic authorities, such as the Police and Fire Department; or to the Eagle Mountain–Saginaw Public Information Office (232-****).

SOURCE: Eagle Mountain–Saginaw Independent School District Crisis Management Plan. Used with permission.

Resource A

Bus Failure

When a school bus is making a route and mechanical failure occurs, drivers:

- Call the Transportation Department for school day breakdowns, 6 a.m. to 6 p.m.
  Transportation Department (827-****).

- Call dispatch number for breakdowns after 6 p.m. (827-**** or 984-****).

- Follow district policy regarding the safety of students.

SOURCE: Spring Branch ISD Crisis Management Plan. Used with permission.

Explosion or Fire

When an explosion occurs in a building, there is an immediate threat to students and staff.

First Actions

- Evacuate the building, taking proper shelter to provide the greatest safety to students and staff.
- Call the Fire Department: 911.
- Call the superintendent: ***-****; ***-**** (home).
- If time permits and if circumstances indicate, call the Boswell Liaison Officer at 237-****, Tarrant County Sheriff's Department (884-****), Saginaw Police Department (232-****), and/or Blue Mound Police Department (232-****).

Preventive/Supportive Measures

- Develop your building evacuation plan for fires and other kinds of building-level disasters and keep a copy of that plan behind this page and in other available files.
- Provide for alternate shelter.

SOURCE: Eagle Mountain–Saginaw Independent School District Crisis Management Plan. Used with permission.

Resource A

Gas Leaks

Natural gas leaks can occur inside or outside of a building. The potential hazards of a gas leak are fire, explosion, carbon monoxide poisoning, and suffocation. You should suspect a gas leak if you smell a very unpleasant odor, like that of rotten eggs. Mercaptan is added to gas to let you know that a leak exists.

For all gas leaks:

- Contact your building principal or designee.
- Contact the Maintenance Department (232-****) and state the emergency situation.
- If Maintenance is not available, and the situation is an emergency, call the Fire Department at 911.

If the smell of gas is faint:

- Open windows or doors.
- Evacuate the area.

If the smell of gas is strong:

- Evacuate the building.
- Move upwind from any smell.

If person(s) is unconscious:

- Do not enter area without breathing protection.
- Remove all persons from area.
- Contact school nurse.

SOURCE: Eagle Mountain–Saginaw Independent School District Crisis Management Plan. Used with permission.

Hazardous Material Spills

There are three major concerns during a spill:
1. Direct contact with the material
2. Indirect contact with the materials, i.e., fumes
3. Appropriate cleanup and disposal

In all spill situations, evaluate the area until cleanup is complete. Notify your building principal or designee immediately. Follow the procedures below.

Direct Contact

- Evacuate the area to avoid fumes.
- Remove contaminated clothing and flush the area with cold running water for 15 minutes. If flushing the eye area, position the flow into the eye while holding the eyes open.
- Notify the school nurse.

Indirect Contact

- Evacuate the area to avoid fumes.
- If the spill is outside, move upwind from the spill.
- Building principal or designee will contact Durham Transportation (847-****), if evacuation from campus is necessary, and/or Maintenance Department at (232-****) to shut down ventilation system that transports fumes.

Cleanup and Disposal

- Never enter a spill area alone.
- Spill areas should be ventilated with fresh air and directional fans that prevents direct exposure.
- Follow cleanup procedures in district guide, "How to Handle a Chemical Spill."

For traffic control: Call the Boswell Liaison Officer (237-****), Sheriff's Department (884-****), Saginaw Police Department (232-****), and/or Blue Mound Police Department (232-****).

Whenever possible, identify the spill to emergency personnel with the following information:
1. Product information
2. Manufacturer information
3. Product contents/ingredients as given on container (whenever possible, spell names to avoid misunderstanding)
4. Volume of spill/exposure
5. Reactions on surface/individuals
6. Product contamination with other chemicals

SOURCE: Eagle Mountain–Saginaw Independent School District Crisis Management Plan. Used with permission.

Resource A

Power Failure or Lines Down in Area

If there has been a power failure at the school, or if lines are reported down in the area of a school:

Power failure:

- Call Maintenance Department (232-****). Although lights will not work on phone, usually the phones will operate.

Lines down in area:

- Have an adult in the area of the downed lines to prevent children and people from going near them.
- Call the power company for your area.
- Call Maintenance Department for backup 232-**** (7:30 a.m.-4:00 p.m.).
- After 4:00 p.m. and before 7:30 a.m. call Tarrant County Sheriff's Department (884-****), Saginaw Police Department (232-****), and/or Blue Mound Police Department (232-****).

SOURCE: Eagle Mountain–Saginaw Independent School District Crisis Management Plan. Used with permission.

Plane Crash on or Near Campus

Determine first if there is an immediate threat to students and staff.

First Actions

- Evacuate the building, taking proper shelter to provide the greatest safety to students and staff.
- Call the Fire Department: 911.
- Call the superintendent: 232-****
  -* (home).
- If time permits and if circumstances indicate, call the Boswell Liaison Officer at 237-****, the Tarrant County Sheriff's Department (884-****), Saginaw Police Department (232-****), and/or Blue Mound Police Department (232-****).

Preventive/Supportive Measures

- Develop your building evacuation plan for fires and other kinds of building-level disasters and keep a copy of that plan behind this page and in other available files.
- Provide for alternate shelter.

SOURCE: Eagle Mountain–Saginaw Independent School District Crisis Management Plan. Used with permission.

Resource A

Serious Injury or Death

- Call the school nurse and/or nurse assistant who will activate the Health Services Emergency Care System and notify the Coordinator of School Health Services.

- Notify the building principal or designee.

- Follow the written campus plan for accidents and emergencies as outlined on the Health Services Emergency Care System flowchart posted in the clinic and main office.

- Refer to Accidents and Medical Emergencies—(Section: Activating the Emergency Care System [IIIA-2]).

- Notify the parent/employee, nearest relative as indicated on the Clinic Emergency Card (*injury only*).

- Call Wayne F. Schaper (464-**** x 2340) or Spring Branch ISD Police Department dispatcher (984-****) *in the event of a death. (Do not notify next of kin.)*

- The building principal or designee will appoint a staff member, along with the Clinic Emergency Card, to follow the ambulance to the hospital. The nurse/nurse assistant should remain on the campus.

- Refer press inquires to the Spring Branch ISD Director of Communications (464-**** x 2272 or 2273). *(Do not issue a statement to the press.)*

SOURCE: Spring Branch ISD Crisis Management Plan. Used with permission.

Flood Disaster Planning

In the cases of flooded streets, the building principal may be notified by the EM-S ISD administration to hold the students at school.

Learn these flash flood terms used by the National Weather Service hydrologic forecasts and warnings:

1. *Flash flood* means the occurrence of a dangerous rise in water level of a stream or over a land area in a few hours or less caused by heavy rain.

2. *Flash flood watch* means that heavy rains occurring or expected to occur may soon cause flash flooding in certain areas and citizens should be alert to the possibility of a flood emergency that will require immediate action.

3. *Flash flood warning* means that flash flooding is occurring or imminent on certain streams or designated areas and immediate precautions should be taken by those threatened.

When a flash flood watch is issued:

1. The building principal or designee should listen to local radio or TV for possible flash warnings and flooding progress.

2. Be prepared to move from danger quickly if required.

3. If you are on a road, watch for flooding in highway dips, low areas, and around bridges.

4. Watch for signs (thunder, lightning) of distant heavy rainfall.

When a flash flood warning is issued:

1. Do not attempt to cross a flowing ditch or stream on foot where water is above your knees.

2. Do not attempt to drive through dips of unknown depths. If your vehicle stalls, abandon it and seek high ground.

3. Be especially cautious when dark, when it is harder to recognize flood dangers.

After the flash flood warning—general:

1. Recognize that flash flooding may have ended, but general flooding may come later in streams and rivers.

2. Know the location of high ground and how to get there.

3. Stay out of flooded areas, streets, and intersections.

SOURCE: Eagle Mountain–Saginaw Independent School District Crisis Management Plan. Used with permission.

Resource A

Hurricane Disaster Planning

Hurricane season falls in the months of June through November. The following information should be helpful in providing for the safety of students and school personnel.

Words of warning:

- *Gale warning* means winds of 38-55 miles per hour.
- *Storm warning* means winds of 55-74 miles per hour.
- *Hurricane watch* means hurricane conditions are a real possibility. Everyone in the area covered by the watch should listen for further advisories and be prepared to act quickly if hurricane warnings are issued.

**Hurricane precautions
(also see Flood Disaster Planning):**

Before a hurricane:

- Designate a safe area of the building where students and faculty should take refuge.
- Assemble survival equipment, which may include a flashlight(s), battery-powered radio, extra batteries.
- School closings will be issued by the superintendent.

During a hurricane:

- Stay calm.
- Keep your battery-powered radio tuned for hurricane advisories and the location of Red Cross shelters.
- Stay inside after rains or winds subside. You may be in the eye of the storm and violent weather will soon return.

After a hurricane:

- Be aware that after the storm passes, there may be downed electrical wires and dangerous debris. Washouts may weaken roads and bridges, which could collapse.
- See Tornado Disaster Planning to be prepared for possible tornadoes after a hurricane.

SOURCE: Spring Branch ISD Crisis Management Plan. Used with permission.

Tornado, Disaster Planning

Local building plans, and the annual school district plan for fire, tornado, or other catastrophic conditions, may be filed and kept for reference immediately following this page.

Inservice education for teachers and staff shall be planned at regular intervals and as needed.

Disaster drills shall be planned and implemented according to EM-S ISD directions at regular intervals and as needed.

Tornado disaster planning:

Several topics of concern need to be considered in districtwide and in building-level development of plans to meet a tornado disaster, or other major catastrophe. These include:

- General principles
- Administrator planning for local buildings
- Responsibilities of teaching staff
- Responsibilities of school administrators
- Responsibilities of custodial staff

Each of the above topics will be discussed on this and the following pages by topic.

Inservice education for staff (and training for students) may be provided at central and local buildings levels. Frequent review of the topics is desirable.

General principles:

Some general principles need to be kept in mind when making either districtwide or building-level disaster plans. They include:

- It is impossible to anticipate all of the situations that may occur; however, there is much planning that may be done before an occurrence of a tornado or other disaster.
- It is impossible to do everything and to completely control all phases of a disaster situation.
- *Each principal* is the key decision maker and is the final authority for the control and safety of all personnel and all students under his or her supervision. The maintenance division may make suggestions to help facilitate disaster planning, as well as offer help after a disaster.

Administrator planning for local buildings:

- Designate the best tornado protective areas in the building by shading in the areas on a floorplan of each individual school. Copies of the plan shall be kept in the Crisis Management Plan notebook.
- Copies also shall be filed with the maintenance office and the Tarrant County Sheriff's Department (884-****), Saginaw Police Department (232-****), and/or Blue Mound Police Department (232-****).
- Plans shall be developed that clearly differentiate between the fire evacuation drill and the tornado disaster drill, or other disaster drills.
- In the event a principal shall be absent or injured, each school shall have a well-developed sequence of authority using professional personnel and/or sectional leaders.

Tornado watch

- A tornado watch shall exist when called by the U.S. Weather Service. This condition occurs when there is a better than normal chance of dangerous weather with damaging winds or one or more tornadoes.
- Generally speaking, signs that usually precede a tornado include one or more of the following:
    1. Severe lightning
    2. Destructive, high winds
    3. Heavy rains
    4. Large, heavy hail
- Report immediately, even your suspicions of, any of the following:
    1. Funnel-shaped, rotating clouds
    2. Protuberance(s) or rotary motion at the base of a thundercloud system
    3. Any rotating cloud of debris or dust near the ground
- If it is too dark to see adequately, listen for any distinctive roar similar to a big jet aircraft or many trains rolling nearby.
- Listen for radio and television reports.

Tornado warning

- If a tornado is spotted or reported in your area, sound the alarm immediately.
- All teachers shall have an accurate class roll or roster with them.
- Move everyone immediately to predesignated area.
- Do not leave a building except to go to a predesignated, safer building unless instructed to do so by the civil authorities in charge; keep abreast of who these civil authorities might be (police, fire department, civil defense).
- If a tornado is spotted or reported as being imminent, assume disaster drill position.

Post-tornado

- If a tornado passes without striking you, be cautious as there may be other funnels in the area. Usually, however, more than one tornado does not occur in the same general path following the initial tornado.
- If your building is struck by a tornado:
  1. Call maintenance to turn off gas and electricity at the main switch(es) as soon as possible.
  2. Activate disaster first aid person/team.
  3. Evacuate damaged area cautiously to prearranged staging area(s).
  4. The injured should be moved as little as possible. All injured should be noted, and all missing should be reported immediately.
  5. Notification of all damage and injury should be made to the administration building as soon as possible by telephone, radio, or special messenger.
  6. Establish a parent-information response team as soon as possible.
  7. Retain students in area until it is considered safe for students to return to class, go home, be released to parents, or board school buses.

Responsibilities of teaching staff:

Responsibilities of the members of the teaching staff are defined by nature of the tornado emergency as follows:

Resource A

Pre-tornado

- Develop a knowledge and an understanding of the characteristics of a tornado by reading and teaching about them.
- Become thoroughly familiar with your school's plan for your room and your neighbors' rooms.

Tornado watch

- Be alert to developing situations.
- Keep your class roll book ready
- Stay calm. Continue with class assignments.

Tornado warning

- Keep calm. Establish an appearance of confidence. Speak slowly, softly, and distinctly.
- Move rapidly, but in an orderly way, to the designated shelter area for your room. Maintain full control.
- Take your roll book with you.
- Turn out the lights and close the door upon leaving your classroom.
- Make sure that all children have assumed the required safe position before taking your own position.
- Wait until you've been assured that the tornado has passed.

Post-tornado

- Take roll of class and report all injured or missing.
- If possible, return to classroom, do so in an orderly fashion.
- If not possible to return to classroom, wait for instructions from designated authorities.

Responsibilities of school administrators:

The responsibilities of local building administrators, and central administrators, shall be to:

- Maintain overall responsibility. While the Central Office, the Fire Marshal, and the Office of Emergency Preparedness can give information and can help with overall planning for disasters, the final planning authority and action is up to the principal of each individual building.

- Maintain a private number for exclusive use of the principal and other administrators in an emergency.
- Keep currently informed about weather conditions.
- Develop a response group of assistants, spotters, first aid team members, section leaders, and line-of-authority professionals before your first drill is held.
- Establish lines of authority for relaying requests and information to the proper authorities.

For central dispersal or dissemination of news and information, keep the superintendent's office fully informed: 232-****.

Hotlines: _____

- Establish a pattern for who is in charge in case the building's administrative offices are struck by a tornado. This plan shall also include an alternate command post in another part of the building or in another building nearby.

Responsibilities of custodial staff:

Among the responsibilities of members of the custodial staff of a building during tornado and other disasters shall be:

- Become thoroughly familiar with the school's or building's tornado and other disaster plan(s).
- Assist in any way possible to keep disaster equipment in place and in good working condition.
- Prior to and during a tornado, or other disaster:
  1. Assist in preparations wherever possible.
  2. Go to your designated shelter at signal.
  3. If your building is struck by a tornado,
     a. Call Maintenance Department (232-****) to turn off gas and electricity at main switch(es) and connection(s).
     b. Report to the principal and offer your assistance.
     c. Cooperate with Police and Fire Department personnel in any way possible.

SOURCE: Eagle Mountain–Saginaw Independent School District Crisis Management Plan. Used with permission.

Resource A

Bomb Threats, Telephone Threats, and Other Disruptive Demonstrations

The principal must evaluate the seriousness of bomb threats or other disruptive types of demonstrations using input from all sources; then, the principal acts in such a manner that reflects the best safety and interests of those under his or her charge.

Bomb and other threats may be originated in writing, in person, over the telephone, or relayed through a second source.

Basic Documentation

- Don't hang up on phone threats; try to keep caller talking; notify principal; attempt to institute a trace through civil authorities, such as police, or through the phone company.

- Document the phone threat using the Threat Call Checklist immediately following these instruction pages; place copies of the bomb threat sheet at switchboard and other appropriate phone locations.

- Document in writing, as soon as possible, other types of threat contacts including:

    1. Specific time message is received
    2. Date and day of week
    3. Exact wording of message
    4. Estimation of sex, race, age, cultural background of person making threat
    5. Explanation of circumstances under which message is received noting usual, as well as unusual, circumstances such as noises, clothing, actions of persons

Authorities to be involved:

- Spring Branch ISD Police Department   984-****
- Executive director for administration   464-**** x 2340

SOURCE: Spring Branch ISD Crisis Management Plan. Used with permission.

Telephone Threats

Telephone threats are made against individuals or buildings. Threats should be considered serious, and they should be handled in a calm and consistent manner.

Threats to individuals:

- Keep the caller engaged on the telephone, if possible, and call the Tarrant County Sheriff's Department (884-****), Saginaw Police Department (232-****), and/or Blue Mound Police Department (232-****).

- Make a record of the call using the Threat Call Checklist form provided under Bomb Threats in this plan.

Threats to buildings:

- Keep the caller talking on the telephone; meanwhile, contact the Tarrant County Sheriff's Department (884-****), Saginaw Police Department (232-****), and/or Blue Mound Police Department (232-****).

- Remain calm. Make a record of the call immediately using the Threat Call Checklist form provided.

- When time permits, call the superintendent (232-****).

SOURCE: Eagle Mountain–Saginaw Independent School District Crisis Management Plan. Used with permission.

Resource A

Threat Call Checklist

Don't hang up phone. (Use another phone to call police.)

Time of call _____

Record the exact words used by caller: _____

_____

_____

_____

Ask:

What time is it set for? _____

Where is it? _____

What does it look like? _____

Why are you doing this? _____

Who are you? _____

Voice on phone: (check list) ☐ Man ____ ☐ Woman ____ ☐ Child ____
☐ Intoxicated ____ ☐ Speech impediment ____ ☐ Accent ____
☐ Other _____

Background noise (check list) ☐ Music ____ ☐ Children ____ ☐ Talk ____
☐ Airplane ____ ☐ Traffic ____ ☐ Typing/computer ____
☐ Other _____

Don't hang up phone. (Use another phone to call Spring Branch ISD Police Department 984-****.) Person receiving call, immediately notify the building principal/person in charge and alert superintendent's office.

Date _____ Call received by _____

Distribute copies *immediately* as shown below:

cc: Building principal
 Superintendent's office
 Spring Branch ISD Police Department

SOURCE: Spring Branch ISD Crisis Management Plan. Used with permission.

Child Kidnapping

Preventive activities that may help avoid child kidnapping situations are:

- School secretary should have at her desk a list of students who are not to be released to anyone except a particular parent or guardian.

- Enrollment cards of such students should be red-flagged.

- Before releasing a child to anyone except the parent or guardian on the list, the school secretary should check with the custodial parent and/or guardian for approval; a record of the time and date of phone approval should be made and kept.

- When a parent telephones a request that a child be released from school, the identity of the caller should be confirmed (by a separate call to the parent or guardian, if needed) before the child is permitted to leave. In the event of any doubt, the message and phone number should be written down; a return call should be made after cross-checking the phone number with those on file in the child's folder or on the emergency card.

In the event of child kidnapping:

- Notify the principal.

- Call the parent/guardian listed on the student's emergency card.

- Call the superintendent and keep him informed of developments.

- Call the Tarrant County Sheriff's Department (884-****), Saginaw Police Department (232-****), and/or Blue Mound Police Department (232-****).

- Do not release any information to the press. Refer requests for information to the Eagle Mountain–Saginaw ISD Public Information Office (232-****).

SOURCE: Eagle Mountain–Saginaw Independent School District Crisis Management Plan. Used with permission.

Resource A

Custody Laws Affecting the School

Request to Release Child

- Divorced parents

    1. Refuse to release child except to the custodial parent. An exception can be made only upon the written request of the custodial parent. Written request shall be kept on file.

    2. A change in custody should be noted with a copy of the court order or court document and kept on file.

- Separated parents

    Release to either parent unless there is on file a notarized statement from the parent-in-residence.

Request to See Child at School

- Divorced parents

    Contact custodial parent and abide by the expressed wishes of that parent.

- Separated parents

    Permit either parent to visit.

Medical Emergency

- Divorced parents

    1. Use emergency information listed on student's card.

    2. Do not contact noncustodial parent.

- Separated parents

    1. Use emergency information listed on the student's card.

    2. Either parent may be contacted.

SOURCE: Spring Branch ISD Crisis Management Plan. Used with permission.

Missing or Runaway Child

**If a child becomes lost or is suspected of
being a runaway between home and school:**

- Check with parent if child does not arrive at school and has not been reported absent.

- Call building principal and give child's possible route to school.

- Advise parent to notify police if student has been located within a reasonable period of time. Note: This notification to the police must be made be a parent.

**If a child leaves school or is reported
missing between school and home:**

- Call parent or guardian.

- Call building principal.

- Call police if student has not been located within a reasonable period of time. *Note:* It is important to maintain one contact person at the Tarrant County Sheriff's Department (884-****), Saginaw Police Department (232-****), and/or Blue Mound Police Department (232-****).

In both of the above situations:

- Call the superintendent (232-****).

- Call the Tarrant County Sheriff's Department (884-****), Saginaw Police Department (232-****), and/or Blue Mound Police Department (232-****).

- Refer calls of inquiry from the media/press to the EM-S ISD Public Information Office (232-****).

SOURCE: Eagle Mountain–Saginaw Independent School District Crisis Management Plan. Used with permission.

Resource A

Children Left at School

Each campus/department will develop procedures for children left at school or other school-sponsored activities. District employees should be familiar with notification procedures for contacting district administrators.

1. Check the student's emergency card and call the parents. *Do not* transport child in private vehicle unless authorized.

2. Call building principal or designee at school or at home.

3. Call the Tarrant County Sheriff's Department (884-****), Saginaw Police Department (232-****), and/or Blue Mound Police Department (232-****), if the parent cannot be reached.

SOURCE: Eagle Mountain–Saginaw Independent School District Crisis Management Plan. Used with permission.

Loitering In or Around Building

Loitering in a school building, on a school campus, or near a school campus is a misdemeanor and is covered under Education Code 4.23.

Procedures to follow when persons are suspected of loitering include:

- Strangers on campus should be approached in pairs. Have another staff member present when you approach the loiterers, ask for identification, determine the nature of their presence, and direct and/or accompany them to the proper office.
- If they have no acceptable purpose, ask them to leave.
- If they refuse to leave, ask them once more to leave and remind them they are in violation of the law and that the police will be called.
- If they continue to refuse to leave, call the Tarrant County Sheriff's Department (884-****), Saginaw Police Department (232-****), and/or Blue Mound Police Department (232-****) and have them removed.

SOURCE: Eagle Mountain–Saginaw Independent School District Crisis Management Plan. Used with permission.

Resource A

Stranger on Campus

Measures preventive in nature and intended to control the access of strangers to the building may include:

- Entrances to the school should be kept locked during the school day to ensure use of main entrances by school visitors.

- Post decals at building entrances asking visitors to the building to go to the office and identify themselves.

- Buildings should be properly marked (by readable maps posted near entrance or by signs) giving directions to office.

- Building teachers, administrators, and staff should approach, greet, and direct visitors to the proper office.

- Direct strangers who fail to identify themselves or their business at school to leave the campus immediately.

- Notify the Boswell Liaison Officer (237-****), the Tarrant County Sheriff's Department (884-****), Saginaw Police Department (232-****), and/or Blue Mound Police Department (232-****).

- *Special Note:* Loitering on a school campus or in a building or near a school campus is a misdemeanor and is covered under Texas Education Code 4.23.

SOURCE: Eagle Mountain–Saginaw Independent School District Crisis Management Plan. Used with permission.

Sexual Assault/Sexual Harassment

Sexual Assault Suspected

- If emergency medical attention is needed, administer proper first aid and call 911.

- Once you feel a sexual assault has occurred, contact your building administrator and local law authorities as soon as possible.

- Keep a written record of all calls made regarding the issues, and document signs and suspicions in writing.

- The administrator is responsible for contacting the parent/guardian if a student is involved. The administrator should also contact the superintendent.

- The administrator should follow up on the condition of the assaulted person.

Sexual Harassment Suspected

- Contact your building principal and apprise him or her of the situation. If the situation possibly involves an administrator on campus, contact appropriate authorities at central office.

- If deemed necessary, a formal complaint may be submitted to the assistant superintendent for human resources.

SOURCE: Eagle Mountain–Saginaw Independent School District Crisis Management Plan. Used with permission.

Resource A

Security Breach/Vandalism

When a security breach and/or act of vandalism is discovered in a school district building or within the building grounds area, the following procedures are to be followed in the chronological order listed:

Procedures for Intruder Building Penetration

- If an intruder has penetrated building space, the Tarrant County Sheriff's Department (884-****), Saginaw Police Department (232-****), and/or Blue Mound Police Department (232-****) should be contacted by the building principal or designee.

- If the intruder is still in the building, all personnel must avoid contact with the intruder. Supplying pertinent intruder information to the police is essential.

Procedures for Building Vandalism by Intruder

- If vandalism has occurred inside the building by an intruder (or if damage is extensive to the building and/or its contents or to the building grounds area), the Tarrant County Sheriff's Department (884-****), Saginaw Police Department (232-****), and/or Blue Mound Police Department (232-****) should be informed by the building principal or designee as to the kind, extent, location, and approximate time the damage was incurred.

- Before police arrival, the building space affected should be sealed off by appropriate means and all items within the affected area must be left intact for possible police investigatory procedures.

- Within the limitations of the above, all possible efforts should be expended by building personnel to make emergency repairs to items deemed dangerous to persons or property within the building.

- The building principal or designee should make a record of the type and extent of damage to the building and its contents.

- Call Custodial Services if cleanup help is needed.

- Call Maintenance Department (232-****) if building damage needs immediate repair.
- *Special Note:* If communication is needed after regular working hours, calling the Tarrant County Sheriff's Department (884-****), Saginaw Police Department (232-****), and/or Blue Mound Police Department (232-****) dispatcher will elicit assistance from designated on-duty personnel.
- A maintenance request form detailing pertinent damage information will be forwarded to the Maintenance Department to effect damage repair. If building or content damage has produced safety, security, or educational process problems, immediate telephone contact with Maintenance Department is essential.
- The building principal or designee will note all pertinent information on a Burglary/Vandalism Report, with a copy forwarded to the chief of police for proper evaluation of affected fixed assets items.

Procedures for Outside Building Vandalism by Intruder

- Follow procedures above as appropriate to the situation.

SOURCE: Eagle Mountain–Saginaw Independent School District Crisis Management Plan. Used with permission.

Resource A

Gang or Cult Activity

If you have reason to suspect that a student may be involved in gang activity, procedures in the following sequence should be followed:

- Be knowledgeable of the warning signs of gang/cult involvement (just one sign by itself is not significant).
- Interview the student.
- Document all information relating to gang involvement (even if it does not appear relevant at the time). Notify the Tarrant County Sheriff's Department (884-****), Saginaw Police Department (232-****), and/or Blue Mound Police Department (232-****).
- Keep an open mind.
- Stay objective.
- Notify principal.
- Contact parent for parent conference.

Note: The district's D.A.R.E. officer and/or liaison officer can be contacted to help in the identification of gang signs/activities.

SOURCE: Eagle Mountain–Saginaw Independent School District Crisis Management Plan. Used with permission.

Suspicion or Possession of Alcohol

If you have due cause to believe that a student is in possession of alcohol, take the following steps to determine whether or not the student does actually possess alcohol:

- Bring the student to the office.
- Have two people present.
- Tell the student what you suspect and ask the student to produce the alcohol. If the student refuses, ask the student to empty the contents of his or her pockets, purse, or other containers. Search locker if needed.
- If alcohol is found, notify the parents and enforce the school district's Discipline Management Policy.

SOURCE: Spring Branch ISD Crisis Management Plan. Used with permission.

Resource A

Suspicion or Possession of a Controlled Substance

If you have due cause to believe that a student may be in possession of a controlled substance, procedures in the following sequence shall include:

Teacher/employee:

- If possible, escort the student to the office with his or her possessions.
- Contact the school office to have an administrator come to your classroom.

Administrator:

- Have two people present.
- Tell the student what you suspect and ask the student to empty the contents of his or her pockets, purse, or other containers. Lockers and vehicles may need to be searched also.
- If a controlled substance is found or you think a substance found may be a controlled substance, call Boswell Liaison Officer (237-****), Tarrant County Sheriff's Department (884-****), Saginaw Police Department (232-****), and/or Blue Mound Police Department (232-****).
- Notify the parents or guardians and enforce the school district's Discipline Management Plan as outlined in the student handbook.

SOURCE: Eagle Mountain–Saginaw Independent School District Crisis Management Plan. Used with permission.

Guidelines for Infectious Diseases

General statement: Guidelines for all school personnel are meant to provide simple and effective precautions against transmission of disease for all persons potentially exposed to the blood or body fluids of any individual. No distinction is made between body fluids from persons with a known disease and those from persons without symptoms or with an undiagnosed disease.

Body fluids: The body fluids of all persons should be considered to contain potential infectious agents and should be treated cautiously. The term *body fluids* includes: blood, semen, vaginal secretions, breast milk, feces, urine, vomitus, respiratory secretions, drainage from cuts, tears, and saliva.

Use of gloves: Gloves should be worn by any caretaker with open hand lesions, and when cleaning up blood spills, vomitus, urine, feces, semen, or vaginal secretions. Gloves should also be worn when removing any body fluid spills from the environment, (e.g., furniture, floors, rugs, etc.).

Handwashing: Handwashing after contact with an individual is routinely recommended only if physical contact has been made with the person's blood or body fluids. If unanticipated skin contact occurs where gloves may not be immediately available, hands and/or other affected skin areas of all exposed persons should be routinely washed with soap and water after direct contact has ceased. In the case of accidental contact with blood, hands and/or affected skin areas should be washed immediately. Proper handwashing requires the use of soap and water and vigorous washing under a stream of running water for approximately 10 seconds. A waterless hand rinse should be used when running water is not available.

Cleaning methods: Soiled environmental surfaces should be promptly cleaned with a freshly prepared household chlorine bleach solution (1:10 dilution). Apply a disinfectant absorbent agent to soiled rugs, allow to dry, sweep up with a dustpan and broom, and follow with a disinfectant rug shampoo applied with a brush. Using fresh bleach solution, soak mops, brooms, and brushes for 10 minutes. Other cleaning equipment should also be thoroughly rinsed in fresh bleach solution.

Resource A

Washable clothing should be presoaked and washed separately using one-half cup chlorine or nonchlorine bleach per wash cycle. All district-owned garments must be appropriately cleaned before issued to students. Intimate apparel or garments worn without underclothing will not be reissued to another student.

Material involving direct oral contact, e.g., instrument mouthpieces, CPR manikins, and face masks, should be cleaned before reuse or reissue. Established guidelines for CPR should be followed. If bleaching or immersing the item is contraindicated, scrub surfaces with alcohol (70%) and allow to remain wet for 30 seconds before wiping dry. Surfaces cleaned with bleach solution should remain wet for 10 minutes before rinsing with fresh water and wiping dry.

Disposal of materials: Clothing and other nondisposable materials that are soaked with body fluids should be placed in plastic bags and instructions for handling given to appropriate persons. Disposable towels, tissues, gloves, and cleaning supplies should be used whenever possible, and should be placed in a plastic bag, securely tied, and disposed of daily. Used cleaning solutions should be flushed down a toilet.

SOURCE: Spring Branch ISD Crisis Management Plan. Used with permission.

Suicide

KNOWLEDGE OF INTENT

I. The principal or designee will verify intent and depending upon circumstances take appropriate action:
   A. Notify school counselor, nurse, etc. for intervention and the development of postintervention strategies.
   B. Notify superintendent's office (232-****).
   C. Contact parent and/or guardian.
   D. Ensure that student is not left alone.

Levels of Suicide Risk

Priority 2:

This individual has:
   a. vague feelings of not wanting to go on, hopelessness, despair, or depression.
   b. no real concrete or immediate suicide plan, or one that is difficult to execute.
   c. made no explicit threats.
   d. the ability to escalate to a medium or high risk.
   e. the greatest opportunity to benefit from supportive discussion, monitoring, and primary intervention.
   f. some support person available.
   g. no means of suicide in his or her possession.
   h. not yet experienced a total lack of success in everyday activities.

Priority 1:

This individual has:
   a. made direct explicit suicide threats.
   b. the means of suicide close at hand.
   c. a well-developed suicide plan.
   d. made final arrangements.
   e. no perceivable support person.
   f. experienced serious, real, or perceived losses in the past year.
   g. decided that death is his or her only option.
   h. experienced failure in all areas of his or her life.
   i. either severe depression or is calm if decision has been made.
   j. made explicit statements of desire to die.

Resource A

KNOWLEDGE OF ATTEMPT

I. The principal or designee will:
   A. Treat attempted suicide as a medical emergency and call 911 (the police officer on call will follow regulations authorized by his or her police department).
   B. Should the suicide be completed, designate a person to secure the area until arrival of police officer and other responding units.
   C. Contact superintendent's office (232-****).
   D. Contact parent/and or guardian in all cases.

II. The superintendent will:
   A. Dispatch the district's Crisis Management Team.
   B. Notify other appropriate central administrators/Board members.
   C. Notify Public Information Office

III. The Crisis Management Team will:
   A. Dispatch counselors to the scene.
   B. Present information to parent/guardian for obtaining appropriate services in the community.

IV. The Public Information Office will:
   A. Meet with superintendent and other administrators to gather factual information.
   B. Release appropriate information to the appropriate persons (staff, students, media, etc.)

SUICIDE QUESTIONNAIRE[1]

It is very important to confer with the student to gather firsthand knowledge about his or her suicidal thoughts. The evaluator needs to remain calm and assess the situation in a very thorough manner. The following questions should be asked of the student.

1. How will you do it? (Is the plan vague or specific?)
2. How much do you want to die?   1 little desire   2 moderate desire   3 great desire
3. How much do you want to live?   1 little desire   2 moderate desire   3 great desire
4. How often do you have these thoughts? (Rarely or constantly?)
5. When you are thinking of suicide, how long do the thoughts stay with you? (Are the thoughts under control or is there an uncontrolled impulse?)
6. Do you have someone close to you that you can talk to? (Look for student support group or lifeline.)

7. Have you ever attempted suicide? (A history of suicidal thinking, gestures, or attempts = high risk)

8. How were you planning on doing it? (Look for specifics: choosing a specific time, giving personal possessions to friends, writing a note, or saying "goodbye").

9. On a scale of 1 to 10, what is the probability that you might try to kill yourself?

10. What has happened that makes you feel like you want to end your life? (sources of stress: loss, helplessness, hopelessness?)

Note
1. Suicide Questionnaire—*The School Counselor.*

SUICIDE THREATS AND ATTEMPTS

Legislation regarding suicide prevention programs:

Senate Bill 1122 became law and went into effect September 1, 1985. This law deals with the consent of a minor to counseling by a physician, psychologist, counselor, or social worker licensed or certified by this state, for treatment of sexual abuse. physical abuse, or *suicide* prevention without the consent of their parents.

The causes of suicide among young people are many and varied. Some of the most common causes are lack of attention, spite or anger, and depression. The most characteristic feature of suicidal persons is the turning in of aggression against self rather than the directing of aggression outward toward the environment.

Intervention—the school counselor may be the best trained and most professional employee available to handle interventions in suicide threats and attempts. Interventions may include:

For a suicide threat:

- Listen. An effort should be made to react and understand the feelings being expressed behind the words. Allow the person to express his or her feelings in a nonjudgmental way.

- Ask directly if the individual has entertained thoughts of suicide. Harm is rarely done by inquiring directly into such thoughts. Discuss it openly and frankly.

- Determine, if possible, the intensity or severity of the suicide threat.

- Parents should be contacted.

- Evaluate the available resources.

Resource A

- Act definitively. A no-suicide contract should be signed.
- If a student refuses to sign a contract, this is to be documented.
- A referral to services in the community should be given to the students and parents.
- Be affirmative and supportive. Strong, stable guideposts are necessary in the life of a distressed individual.
- Do not be misled if the individual admits seriously considering suicide and then makes light of the issue.
- Be a nonjudgmental listener who shows interest and support.
- Do not leave a medium- or high-risk student alone.

The Suicide Prevention Hotline: 1-800-333-4444

SOURCE: Eagle Mountain–Saginaw Independent School District Crisis Management Plan. Used with permission.

Suicide: A National Crisis

It has been estimated that teenagers in this country attempt suicide every 90 seconds and that they succeed every 90 minutes. In the past decade, suicide has become the second leading cause of death among adolescents. Accidents rank first. However, in many accidents, there is no way of determining whether or not the tragedy was deliberate or accidental. So, many accidents may actually be suicides. Over the past decade, figures seem to bear this out, as suicides continue to be on the rise with one government estimate placing the numbers at 5,000 per year for the 15- to 25-year-old age group.

While suicide rates among younger children 5 to 14 years old are not as high, still some estimates indicate that there may be as many as 1,200 attempts per year in that age group.

Why this alarming increase? After all, suicide—whether as an act of honor, martyrdom, saving face, or as an alternative to "capture by the enemy"—has been a part of the world's populations for thousands of years. Not only was suicide common in India long before Christ (the Old Testament mentions it), but ancient classical civilizations regarded suicide as an honorable way to depart this earth.

Early Christian martyrs practiced suicide until the Catholic Church designated it a sin and a crime in the Middle Ages. From World War II, with its Japanese kamikaze pilots, and continuing through today's Islamic Jihad, we see similar examples of how suicide is regarded as an honorable way to serve one's country.

But while suicide has been a part of the history of most countries, it has only been in the last decade that the high rate of adolescent suicide has grown to alarming proportions as a mental health problem.

The majority of these adolescent suicides are Anglo males and involve deadly weapons such as handguns. Teenage males constitute 20% of our country's suicides, while the percentage of females in the same age group is 15% and growing. Suicide has been described as an epidemic in the United States because the rate has more than doubled in the last two decades. The National Center for Health Statistics predicts that the suicide rate among 15- to 19-year-olds will almost double by the year 2000.

Crisis and Anticipated Responses

Adolescents are affected to varying degrees by events that happen to family members, friends, and classmates. In some cases they are even affected by tragedies involving people whom they only know distantly. For instance, a child may relate to another child in his or her age group even though he or she may not know the child personally. Often, a tragic event represents to that child the first realization that "something bad" can really happen, activating fears and feelings of vulnerability.

The degree of response usually depends upon the closeness of the adolescent to the victim, or his or her exposure to the event. A child who witnesses a tragedy will experience a more profound reaction than the one who hears about it.

The definitions of the crisis children and adolescents may experience are dealt with in this section of the Crisis Management Plan. In each case, these definitions are also accompanied by possible responses that can be anticipated.

Suicide: Definitions and Responses

Suicide is defined as the act of taking one's own life voluntarily and intentionally. A suicide may activate another suicide in an adolescent prone to suicide, especially if suicide is viewed as a heroic act, or if the outpouring of grief, memorials, and publicity is viewed as an "attention producer" to the child who is yearning for attention. It sometimes appears to others as a "glamorous solution" to a problem or to an unhappy life. This is one of the main reasons for crisis intervention in schools following suicide.

Responses to anticipate:

- Denial—including refusal to deal with or accept the fact that a suicide has occurred.

- Anger—which may be manifested in blaming oneself or others and in aggressive behavior.

- Crying—which actually may be listed as a response in conjunction with all cases. It is of little significance by itself unless it becomes prolonged and inappropriate.

- Depression—including inability to concentrate, falling grades, loss of interest in activities, sleep disturbances, and feelings of helplessness, hopelessness, and worthlessness.

- Fear—including recurring nightmares.

- Regret—especially the feeling of wishing that he or she had done more to prevent the situation.

- Involvement with drugs and alcohol—a tragedy such as suicide rarely causes or activates drug or alcohol abuse, but it would likely increase such behavior if it already exists.

Warning signs:

Although there is no foolproof checklist for identifying students at risk for suicide, we will present two lists that can greatly assist in the recognition of high-risk students. The presence of one or two signs should be taken seriously, but is not always indicative of immediate potential. However, the presence of any warning sign should be reported to the appropriate resource.

The following list contains the general warning signs that both professionals and laypersons should be familiar with. It is recommended that you thoroughly know this material so that you can be attuned to signs when they first appear. Remember that the presence of any sign is serious, but not necessarily indicative of imminent risk.

- Preoccupation with themes of death or expressing suicidal thoughts
- Giving away prized possessions, making a will, or other "final arrangements"
- Appearance of peace, relief, contentment—especially following a period of unrest. This occurs when the individual has finally made a decision—suicide—a way to finally solve the problem. It often accompanies the second sign listed above
- Changes in sleeping patterns—too much or too little
- Sudden and extreme changes in eating habits, losing or gaining weight
- Withdrawal from family and friends or other major behavioral changes, or the opposite—acting-out behavior such as aggression
- Changes in school performance, lowered grades, cutting classes, dropping out of activities, or loss of interest in activities
- Use of drugs or alcohol
- Recent suicide of friend or relative
- Previous suicide attempt

Teachers are in a unique position to observe students on a daily basis and to have a perception about the regular or normal behavior of each student. With this in mind, the following list is more specific to the needs of teachers.

Signals of depression or pain:

- Loss of interest or pleasure in ordinary activities

- Alienation or withdrawal from social context
- Loss of sense of humor
- Decreased energy, fatigue, restlessness
- Feelings of pessimism, guilt, worthlessness, failure
- Diminished ability to think or concentrate, a drop in grades or performance
- Loss of friends, withdrawal from social contacts
- Frequent physical complaints, trips to school nurse, visits to doctor, sleep disturbances, extreme loss or gain of weight
- Increasing neglect of personal hygiene, appearance
- Humiliating life event

Once you are familiar with the warning signs, it is important to be able to listen and talk effectively with your students. We recognize that some teachers are more comfortable than others in pursuing certain subjects. However, by using the information in this section, each teacher should be able to increase his or her comfort level and ability to effectively intervene.

Before moving to a specific listing of skills and suggestions, we would like to make some general observations about establishing the best conditions for good communications. Generally, it is important to hear what your students are saying; teachers have ample opportunity to listen to the context of student conversations. It is amazing what students will allow teachers to overhear. Obviously, it is easier to talk to a student with whom you have good rapport. Less obvious is the fact that you can develop this rapport by encouraging students to talk with you and by letting them know that you are available. Of course, you should not wait until there is a crisis to begin developing this rapport.

Specific verbal and listening skills:

- Avoid saying or doing things that would stop the flow of the conversation.
- Listen and "tune-in" to what the student has to say, and then in your own words tell the student what you just heard.
- You can communicate that you care and can be trusted by being nonjudgmental. Although you should never say or do anything that would support suicide as an appropriate course of action, you should always accept the student's thoughts and feelings as he or she presents them. Do not reveal shock at anything the student says. At the same time, do not necessarily condone what has been revealed; instead, just listen.

- Encourage students to express their feelings and accept that these feelings are valid.
- If a student's words or actions concern you, say so.
- Be reassuring, confident, and calm.
- If the student seems to be in imminent danger of self-destructive behavior, do not leave the student alone. If in doubt that he or she may be suicidal, see that the student is in the hands of a professional.

Remember that some students open up more easily than others, even among those who are suicidal. Also, some students won't talk to you, but you should trust your intuition when you feel they are at risk.

- The teacher should read a brief statement of information regarding this tragedy to the first-period class. In most cases, this information should be provided by the central administration.
- The teacher should facilitate a brief discussion with the class.
- The teacher should encourage the students to express their emotions by listening and furnishing feedback.

Implementation of a Postcrisis Plan

In the aftermath following sudden death, there is certain to be confusion on the school campus, whether the death was accidental or intentional. After the initial reaction of shock and disbelief, the teacher has a need for accurate information regarding details of the incident and guidance in the method of relating and interacting with students.

- The teacher should lead a discussion in selecting positive alternatives to coping with problems.
- The teacher should recognize that students handle grief in different ways and should be alert to those who need to be referred to the counselor or Crisis Management Team.
- The teacher should realize that for many students, this is the first experience where he or she faces the reality of the possibility of his or her death or that of a "significant other." This will require a discussion of life and death.

Teachers are very sensitive and vulnerable to a crisis situation that affects their campus. In the midst of rumors and chaos, it becomes vitally important that teachers be kept informed. We must keep in mind that teachers also have a need to express their own feelings and to be understood. The following is a list of suggestions for assisting teachers:

- It is recommended that an inservice on adolescent crisis be provided at the beginning of the year.
- Following a crisis, communicate accurate information to the school staff through an emergency faculty meeting or through written communication.
- It is suggested that school counselors or other professionals be made available to the school staff. The counselors will be able to brief the staff on what to expect and provide guidance.
- Teachers should be provided with small-group counseling support throughout the school day as needed. This could be facilitated by the school counselors or outside professionals.

SOURCE: Eagle Mountain–Saginaw Independent School District Crisis Management Plan. Used with permission.

Shooting

Gun in Building

1. Administration is notified that there is a gun in possession on campus.

2. Administration will notify the Tarrant County Sheriff's Department (884-****), Saginaw Police Department (232-****), and/or Blue Mound Police Department (232-****). The school liaison officer or the D.A.R.E. officer can serve as a first responder if available.

3. Law enforcement and administrator should determine if evacuation is necessary if threat of danger is present.

4. Evacuate immediately the area of concern.

5. Advise all personnel to make no attempt to disarm the student unless he or she expresses a willingness to relinquish the possession of the gun.

6. Contact parents of student involved.

7. Establish a line of communication.

8. Inform the Superintendent of Schools and Public Information Office.

9. Turn situation over to the Police Department and offer assistance as needed.

Shooting Involved

1. Follow the above guidelines, administering basic first aid until health care professionals arrive.

2. File necessary charges against persons involved.

SOURCE: Eagle Mountain–Saginaw Independent School District Crisis Management Plan. Used with permission.

Resource A

Weapons on Campus

Suspicion of Possession

If you have cause to believe that a student is in possession of a weapon, you need to take the following steps to determine whether or not the student actually possesses a weapon:

- Notify the Boswell Liaison Officer (237-****), the Tarrant County Sheriff's Department (884-****), Saginaw Police Department (232-****), and/or Blue Mound Police Department (232-****) for dispatching of an officer.

- Have a designated adult or police officer bring the student to the office. The student should bring any books, backpack, purses, etc., that are in his or her possession at the time.

- At least two adults and a police officer should be present at the meeting.

- After the officer is present, the student should be told what is suspected. If the student denies or refuses to turn over the weapon, ask the student to empty the contents of his or her pockets, purse, book bag, or any other containers. If a search of the student's personal possessions yields nothing, two adults and the student will go to the student's locker for a thorough search.

- Further guidelines as enforced in the district's Discipline Management Plan.

Threatening With Weapons

If a student threatens him- or herself or others with a weapon, the following steps should be taken:

- Teachers should remain calm and talk to the student in a calming voice. The teacher should not attempt to confiscate the weapon.

- Send for principal/assistant principal as quickly as possible.

- Call the Boswell Liaison Officer (237-****), the Tarrant County Sheriff's Department (884-****), Saginaw Police Department (232-****), and/or Blue Mound Police Department (232-****). Notify the superintendent (232-****).

SOURCE: Eagle Mountain–Saginaw Independent School District Crisis Management Plan. Used with permission.

Communicating With the Media

In any building-level crisis situation, it is possible that news media will contact the campus office before calling the Communications Department. Principals should confer with the executive director of communications (464-**** x 2272 or 2273) before releasing information.

Building-Level Communications

- The principal is in charge of building-level communications and is the most likely source of reliable and accurate information to the news media.

- The principal may assume the role of chief communicator to the news media, working collaboratively with the executive director of communications.

- In unusual circumstances, the principal may designate one or more persons to provide information to the media.

Central Communications

- Advise the superintendent's office of the crisis.

- If indicated, seek the direct assistance of the executive director of communications (464-**** x 2272 or 2273).

- The Communications Department shall maintain an up-to-date list of news media to be contacted in a crisis situation.

SOURCE: Spring Branch ISD Crisis Management Plan. Used with permission.

Resource A

Parent Procedures for Picking Up Children in a Crisis

In a student handbook and/or in a letter to parents that is mailed early in the school year, the school should inform parents as to the proper procedures to follow in picking up their child in a crisis situation, such as a tornado.

Among the types of information that may be contained in the letter and/or handbook are:

- Specifications indicating that school is one of the safest places that students may be located during most crises, such as tornadoes and other natural disasters.

- Instructions showing that students will be kept at school until the crisis is determined to be over.

- Instructions emphasizing that students will be released to parents who come to get them.

- Instructions emphasizing that when a person other than the parent comes to get a child, the person in charge of the building will be checking with the student first before releasing him or her, that a record is to be kept as to the person picking up the child; and that if there is any doubt that the parent does not want the child released, then the child will be kept at school.

- *Special Note:* Some schools prefer to follow the policy that only persons designated on the enrollment card may pick up students unless there is a phone call, which can be verified, from the parent or guardian.

SOURCE: Spring Branch ISD Crisis Management Plan. Used with permission.

Person/s in Charge When the Principal Is Away

Under district policy and by law, it is understood that the principal of a school is charged with the responsibility for students, professional staff, and additional employees of his or her building. Therefore, it is the responsibility of the principal to designate a *certified person* to assume a portion of that responsibility and to make decisions during a crisis in his or her absence.

Precautionary Action

- The principal shall develop a list of persons in charge of the building in his or her absence. Suggestions include:
    1. *Elementary schools*—assistant principal, counselor, Campus Operations, and/or other *certified* staff member, as designated. Team in the order designated by the principal.
    2. *Secondary schools*—assistant principals in the order designated by the principal; plus, involvement of other key people as designated by the principal.

- It is advisable that the list mentioned above be kept following this information sheet as well as in other accessible locations and files.

- Persons in charge when the principal is away shall have copies of the Crisis Management Plan notebook or shall be made fully aware of locations of all Crisis Management Plan notebooks assigned to the building.

- Teachers and other building staff should be informed as to who is in charge when the principal is away.

- Person/s in charge when the principal is away need to be thoroughly familiar with crisis situations and with use of the Crisis Management Plan notebook.

SOURCE: Spring Branch ISD Crisis Management Plan. Used with permission.

In compliance with GPSR, should you have any concerns about the safety of this product, please advise: International Associates Auditing & Certification Limited The Black Church, St Mary's Place, Dublin 7, D07 P4AX Ireland
EUAR@ie.ia-net.com

www.ingramcontent.com/pod-product-compliance
Lightning Source LLC
Chambersburg PA
CBHW081356290426
44110CB00018B/2396